DRAWING EUROPE TOGETHER

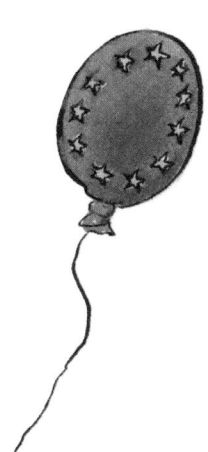

PAN MACMILLAN

First published 2018 by Pan Macmillan
20 New Wharf Road, London N1 9RR
Associated companies throughout the world
www.panmacmillan.com

ISBN: 978-1-5290-1087-9

DRAWING EUROPE TOGETHER

Forty-five Illustrators, One Europe

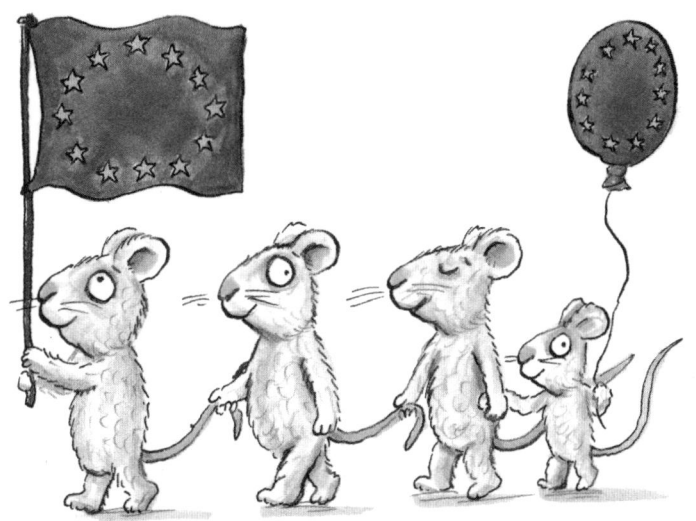

PAN MACMILLAN

Foreword

Europe was named after Europa, a mythological young woman from the eastern shores of the Mediterranean Sea from an area we now call the Middle East. She was kidnapped by a god in the shape of a bull and brought to the place that was later named after her. Today Europe means many things to many people. The seed of this book was planted by a German children's book publisher, Markus Weber at Moritz Verlag, who asked his illustrators to do a 'drawing for Europe'. Whether they wanted to draw something about the story of Europe, the European Union, or anything else on the subject was left completely up to them.

The pictures were first shown during the 2017 Frankfurt Book Fair and afterwards at a government ministry in Berlin – this at the suggestion of German minister Katarina Barley (a woman who has grandparents from four different European nations). In summer 2018, the exhibition came to the UK, thanks to the Institut Français in London, who were able to put it on at very short notice. Some British-based children's book illustrators were asked to contribute, and not surprisingly many commented visually on Brexit. Their drawings are touching and very heartfelt, often full of sadness and anger at the decision to leave the EU. Making children's books requires openness: their creators are citizens of everywhere, just as children are citizens of everywhere. Children love the same stories all over the world – *The Gruffalo* is my witness.

The next step was the addition of contributions from more illustrators to create this book. Although the pictures often speak for themselves, we asked the artists to tell us their thoughts behind the drawings. It seems to me that many of them think the European Union is largely a very good idea and want to express that European unity and collaboration are a good thing.

Personally, Britain has been my home for 36 years. I came to study and work here, and that was made possible by the EU. It has enriched my life and I hope that I have enriched the life of this nation in return by creating *The Gruffalo* and many other popular books together with Julia Donaldson. I've never seen myself as a guest in the UK but it now no longer feels like home to me. The fatal decision of Brexit, which seems to me a tremendous act of national self-harm, fills me with disbelief, pain and anger.

I am aware of the big divisions in this country about the Brexit decision. When I did a workshop with British school children in London, I was very impressed by their own drawings of Europe and the engaged discussion that was triggered by the exhibition. The teacher said, "We should do more of this at school". Perhaps this book will encourage more discussion in schools and among families about history and politics, and the future the children will live in – and that peace and democracy and our way of life should not be taken for granted.

I hope everybody young and old will enjoy this amazing collection of visual statements on Europe and that it will lead to thinking, discussion and *re-thinking*. My personal hope at the time of writing is that it's not too late to change the course of the UK's decision to leave the EU. *Drawing Europe Together* is not just a record of the position taken by myself and many other creators of children's books: it is a document of our time.

Axel Scheffler, 2018

We don't decide where we're born, but we should be able to decide where we call home. Every single family has a structure that has been built up over time. These structures keep changing and growing but they hold us all together no matter where we are from. Why cause instability in our nests, when instead we could continue to connect them and make them stronger?

Marta Altés

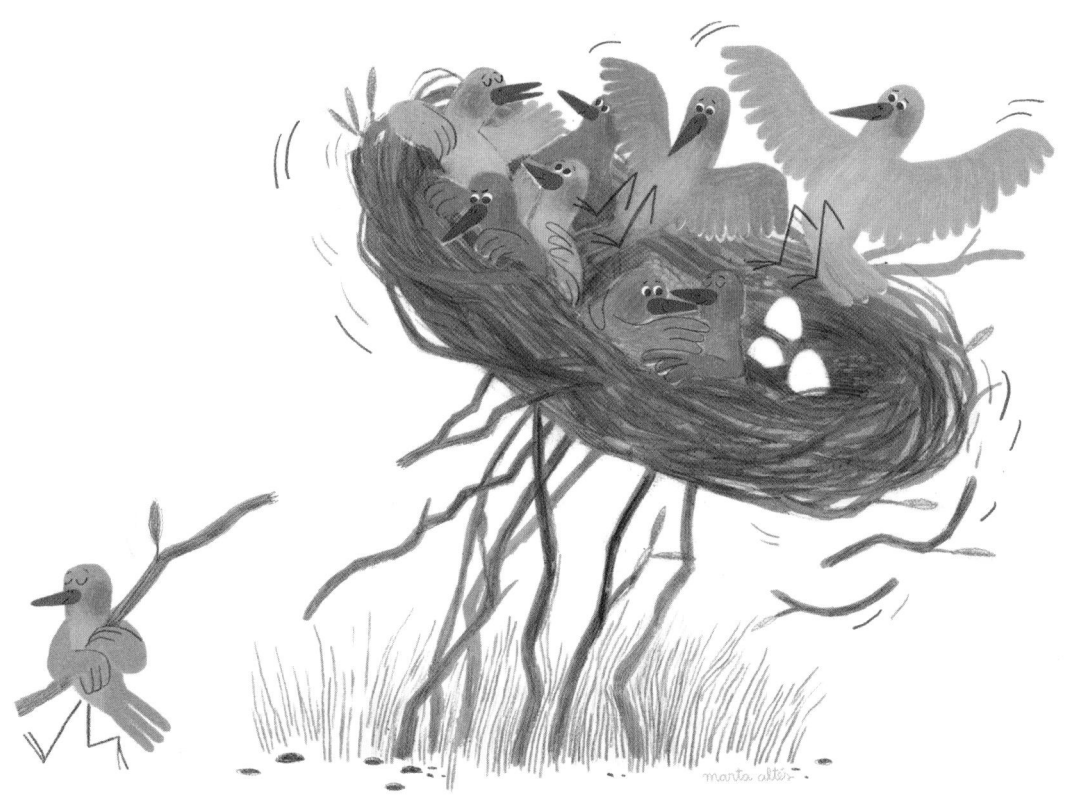

Our Nest

I see Europe as a great feat. It's just like juggling – you have to practise a lot to make it work.

Kristina Andres

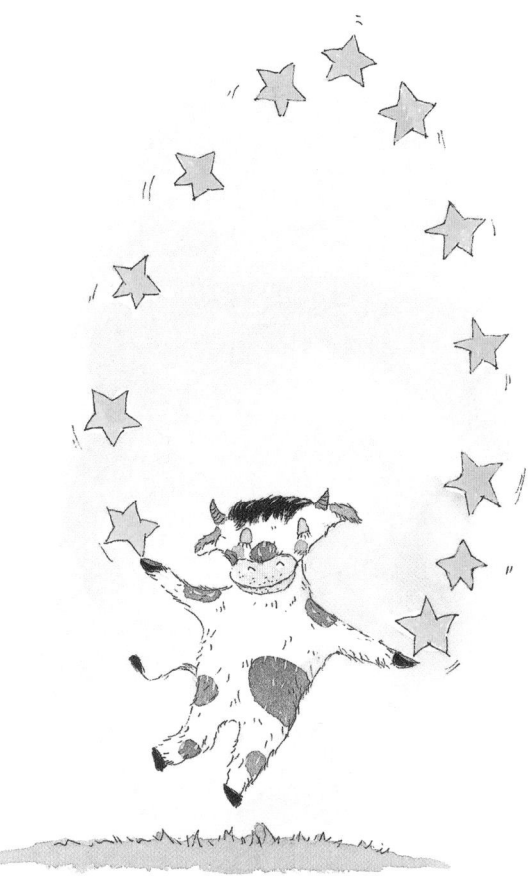

European Dreams

This world can be very confusing at the best of times, especially for children. But I like to think that new generations will continue to learn from history and strive to find ways of securing lasting peace and unity. The European Union was set up to do just that, which might explain why the child in my drawing looks a little baffled.

Steve Antony

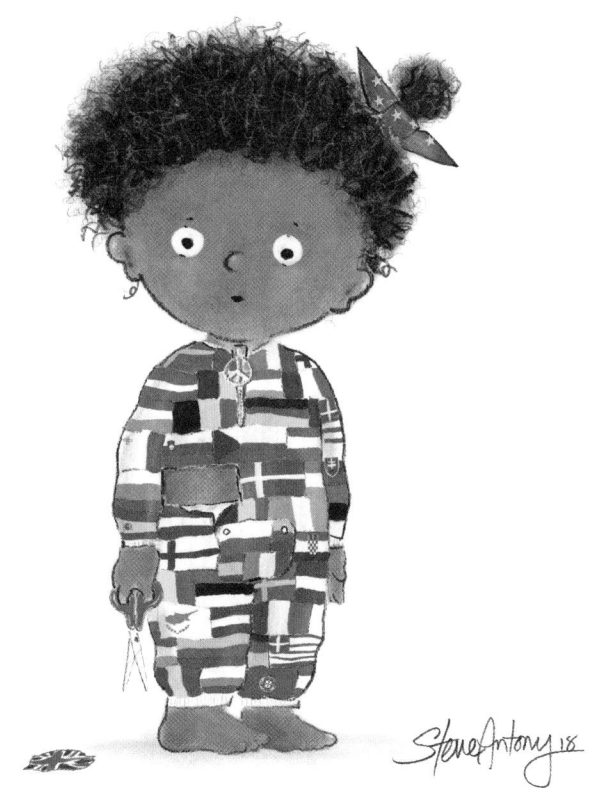

Brexit

For me, the bull is a symbol of lobbying, which has abducted the sceptical Europa. Europe would be better if it were more feminine.

Jutta Bauer

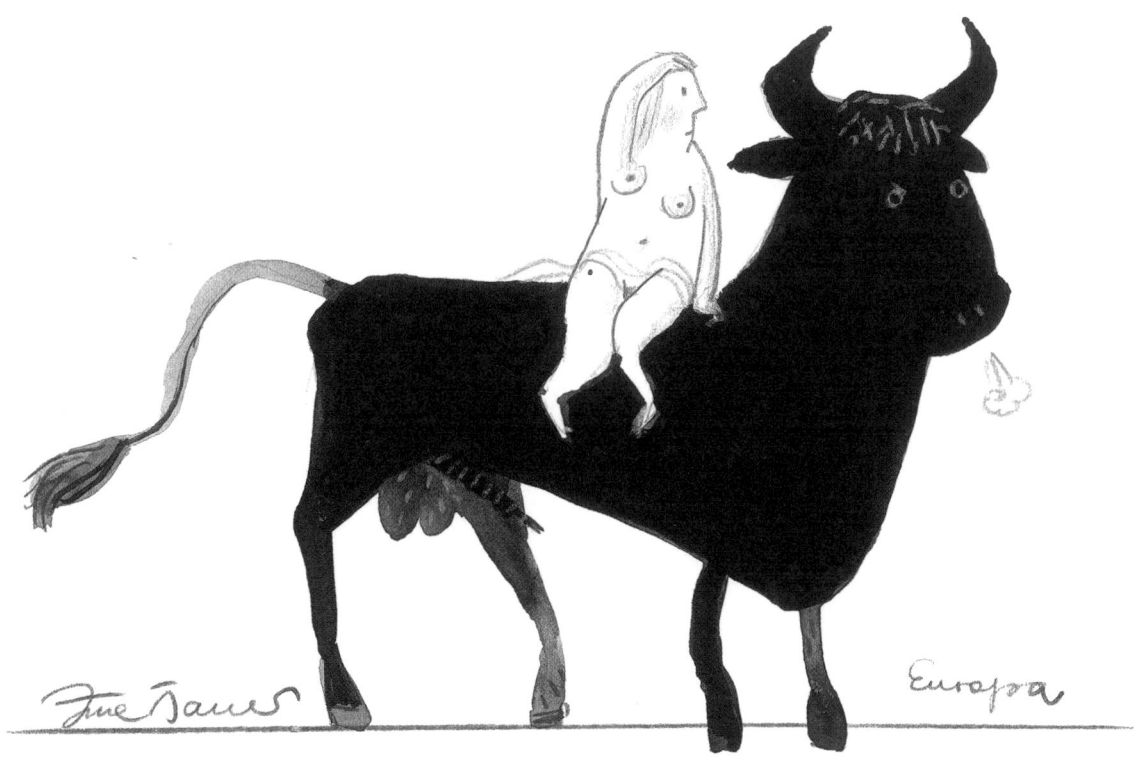

Europa, Sceptical

Music is a unifying force, so I decided to portray each nation as a musical instrument. They are all playing 'Ode to Joy' (the European anthem) together, except for the UK – a lone bugler, looking on forlornly from the sidelines. As H E Luccock once said, "No one person can whistle a symphony. It takes a whole orchestra to play it".

Rob Biddulph

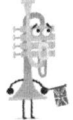

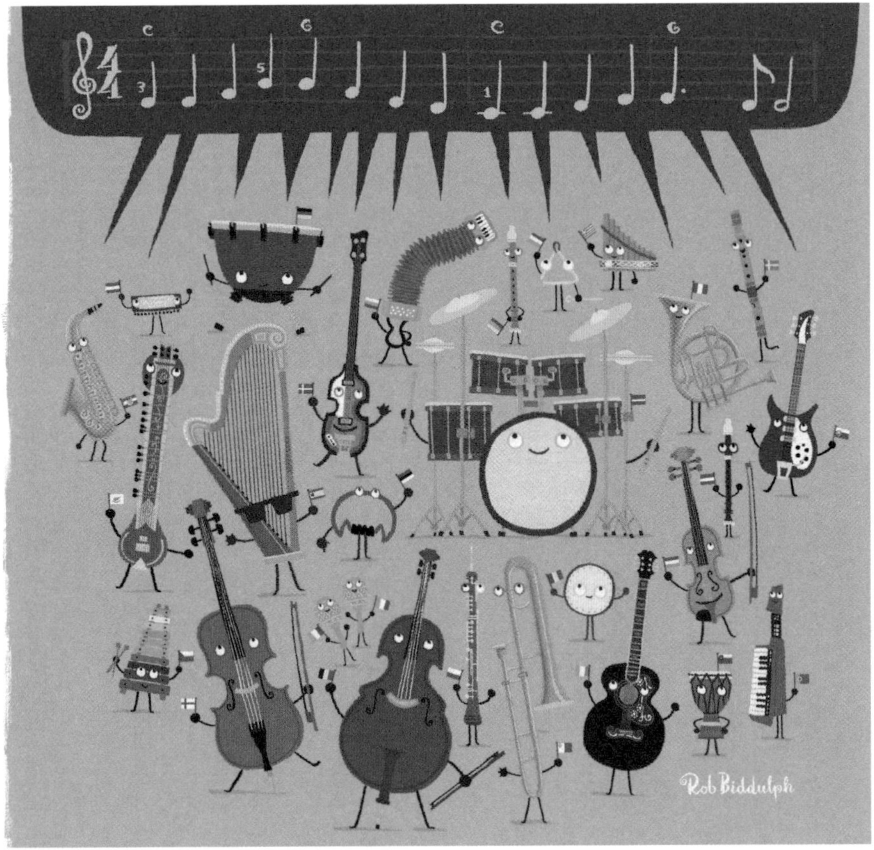

Ode to Joy

I feel privileged to be associated with two institutions that have my name on them; one in Berlin and the other French, though it is in London. As I did the drawing I felt even more European.

Quentin Blake

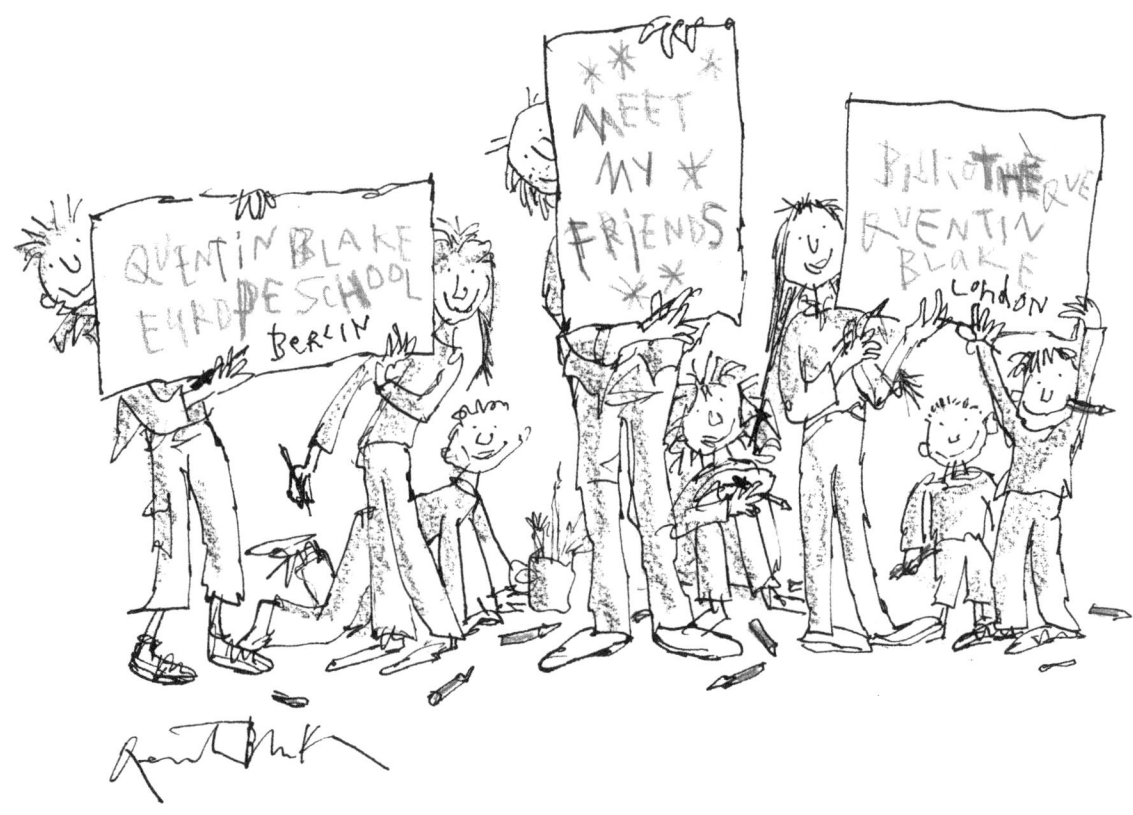

Meet My Friends

Killiok's Song for Europe:

The soft woollen rug we tread with our feet
Wishes it looked more like Nature, its friend.
But one can't quite wash away the tide of a world which keeps
Producing, producing, producing . . . and counting!

Anne Brouillard

Translated by Lionel Tona

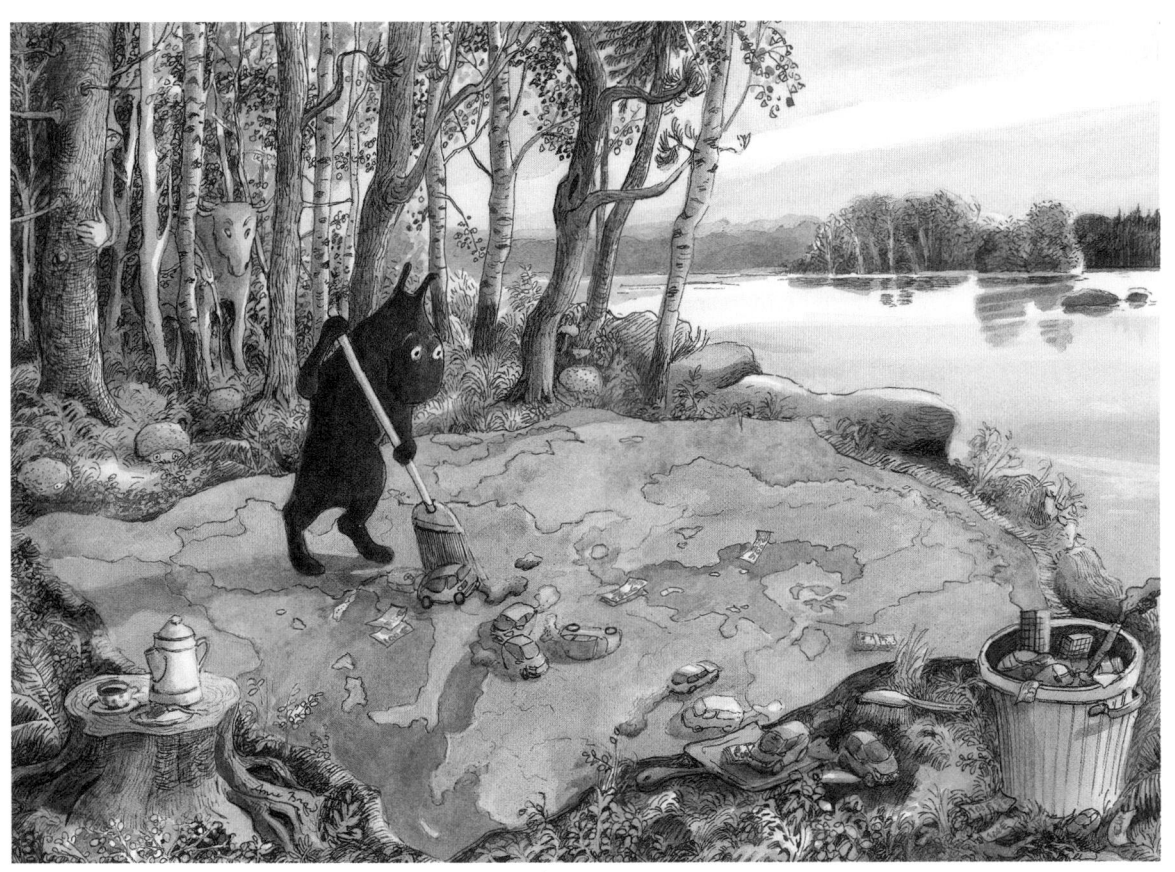

Killiok Takes Care of Europe

This happened with someone I know – not a swivel-eyed loon. He meant well. But why am I the right sort of immigrant? Because I'm white? Because I'm Australian? Because I'm not European? Because you can't actually tell I'm an immigrant? The trouble is, when you make some immigrants unwelcome, all immigrants start feeling unwelcome. This world has enough barriers – we don't need more.

Martin Brown

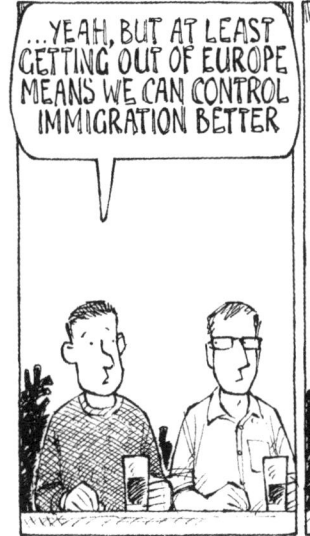
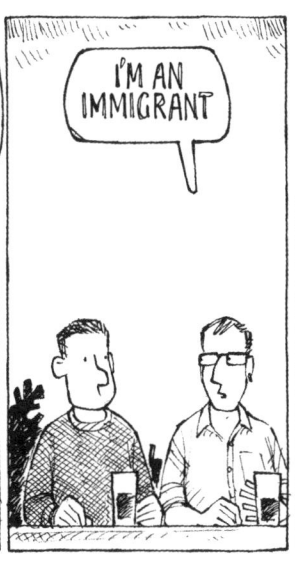
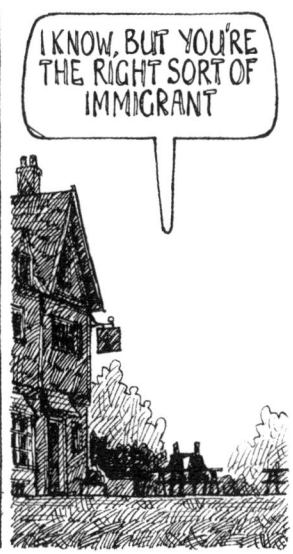
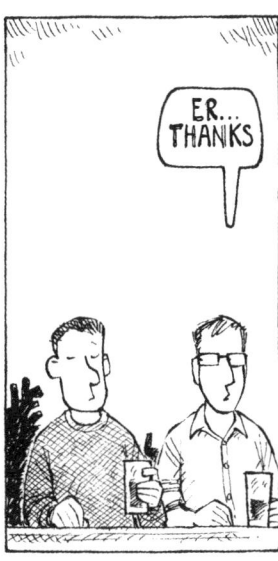

True Story

We've created so much together . . .

Rebecca Cobb

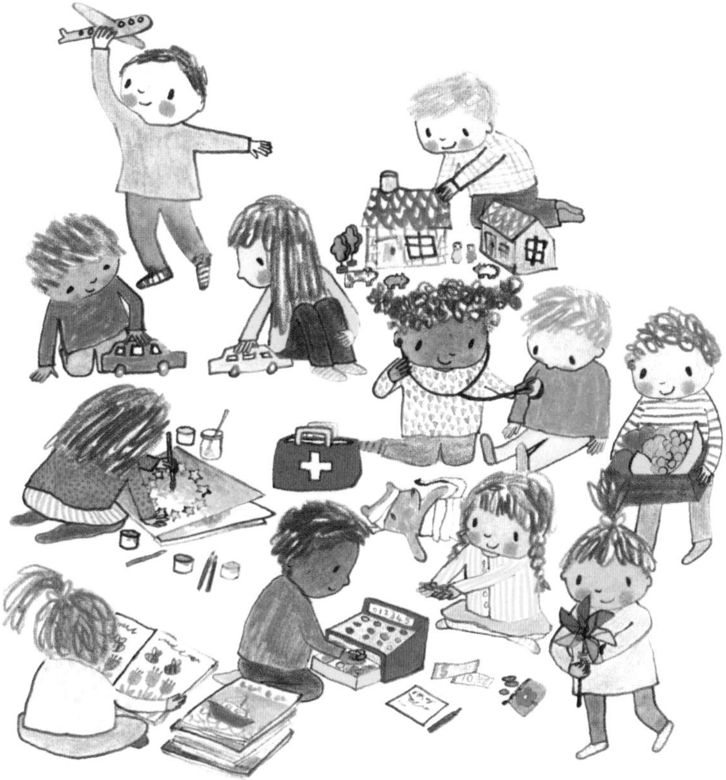

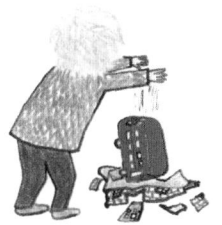

Bus

There is much to be concerned about following the vote to leave Europe. There are so many implications. One of the things I have been most worried about is the effect of impulsive policy-making on the young, who will be consigned to a future decided on for them by those who will not experience the full effects over time. There is no doubt that there was a generational split in the vote to leave the EU. It is a rare fact in the current sea of conjecture. The young voted by a large majority to remain. The vote to leave increased exponentially the older the voter.

The EU is not perfect, but all of us could work to improve things rather than run away. I love being a European. In the end we have to ask ourselves if we can honestly answer a child's question about why we would want to leave our fellow Europeans, when we could stay and work together to improve our collaboration and unity.

Penny Dale

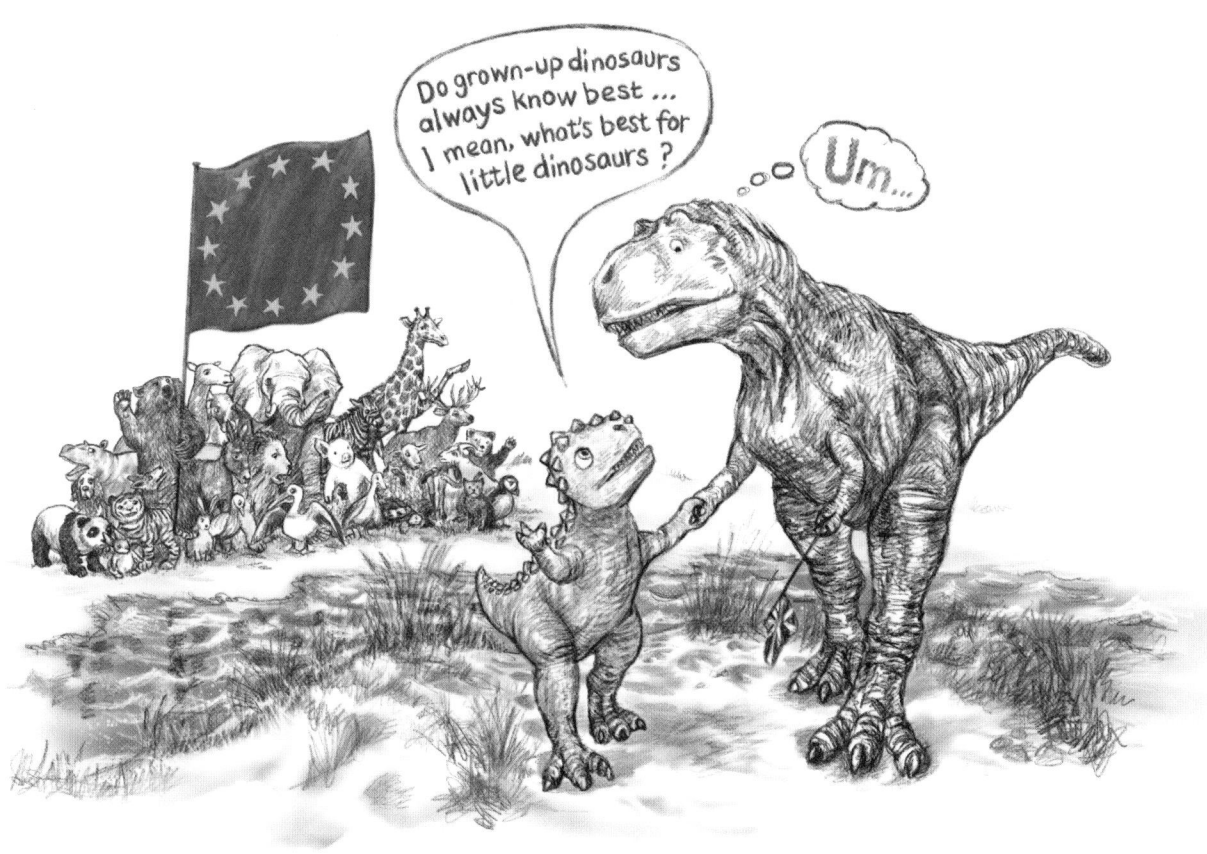

Fair Question

I hope that the door to Europe can be open to people, so that they can bring us new ideas. Together we can achieve a lot.

Antje Damm

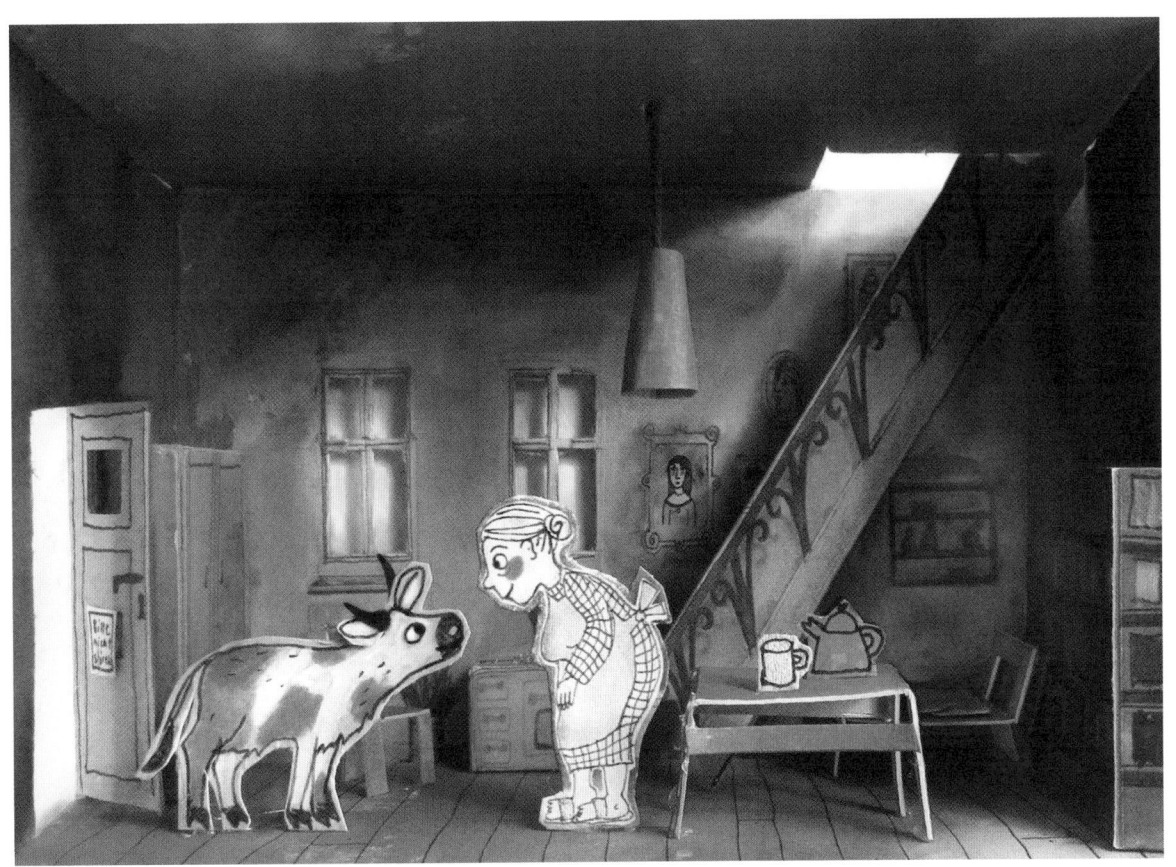

Europe's Fountain of Youth

My drawing is a metaphor for my feelings on the division of the UK referendum. It's perhaps a darker take than many of the other artists' contributions but as a British citizen, I felt an honest one. The eggs represent the stars of the EU flag, our shared values. Something has intruded and undermined that unity leaving us with a feeling of absence and continued uncertainty about what comes next. Hard to believe that at the time of writing we have been living with the result for nearly two years and still it rolls on.

Benji Davies

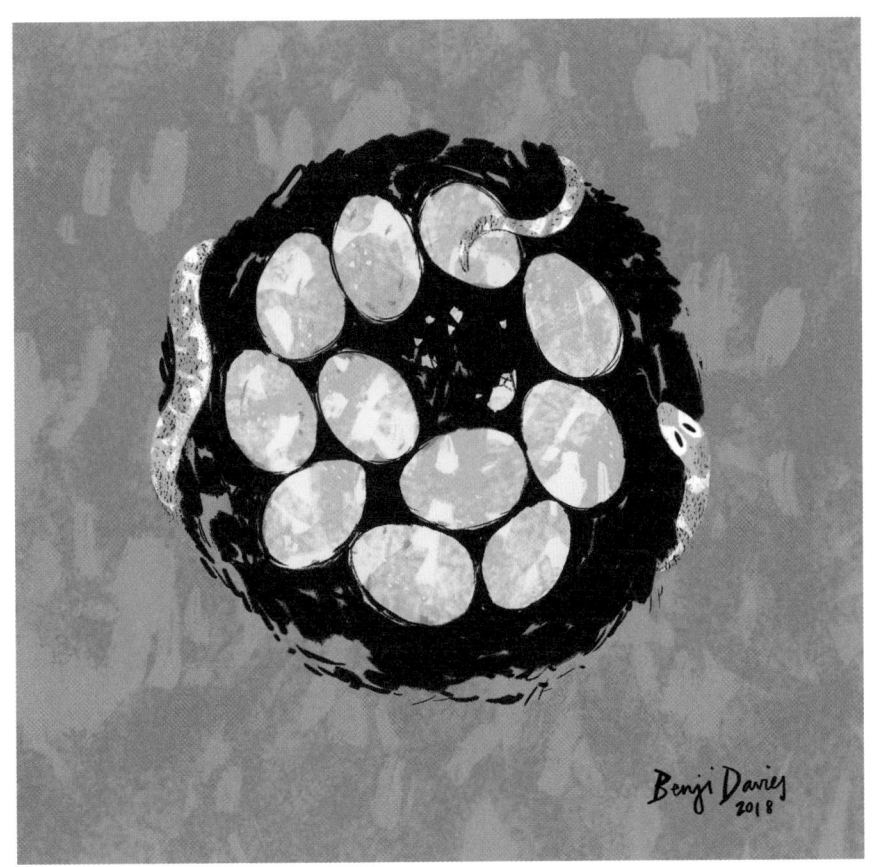

EU Nest

Akim is the emblem of a child in search of peace, hope, respect for each other and the meaning of democracy.

Claude K Dubois

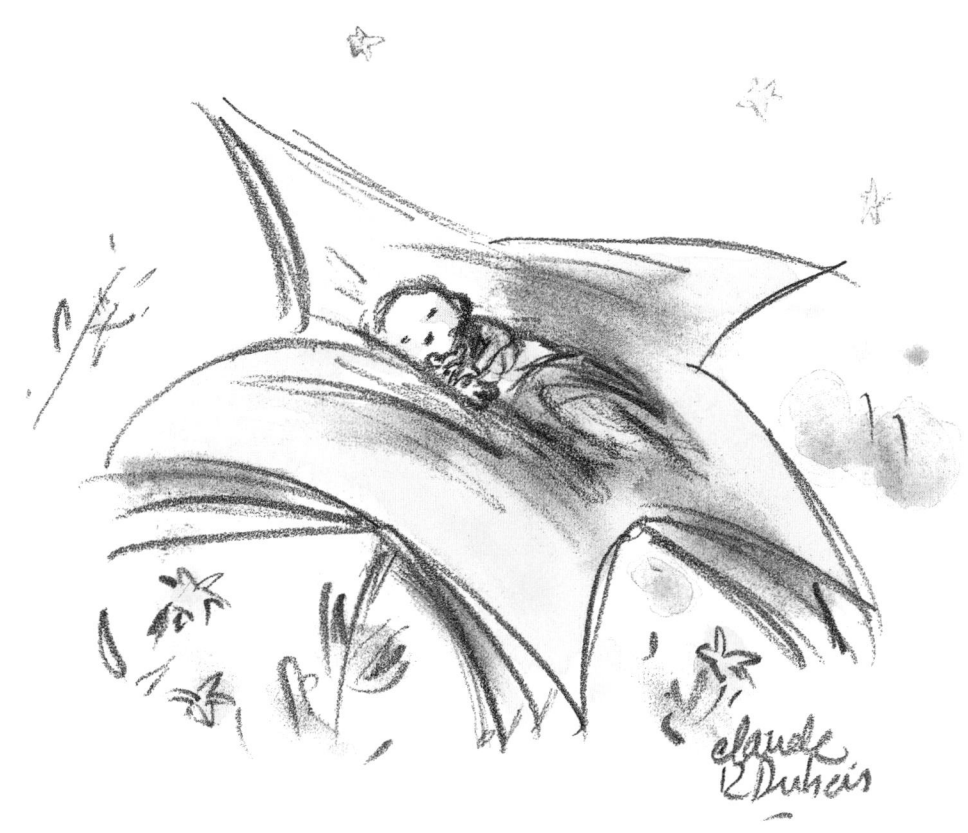

Welcome to Europe, Akim!

As a children's book illustrator it made sense to me to depict the EU countries as children. I was trying to explain Brexit very simply through body language. My three-year-old son asked, "Why doesn't that little boy want to play?". . . it might take me a while to explain.

Polly Dunbar

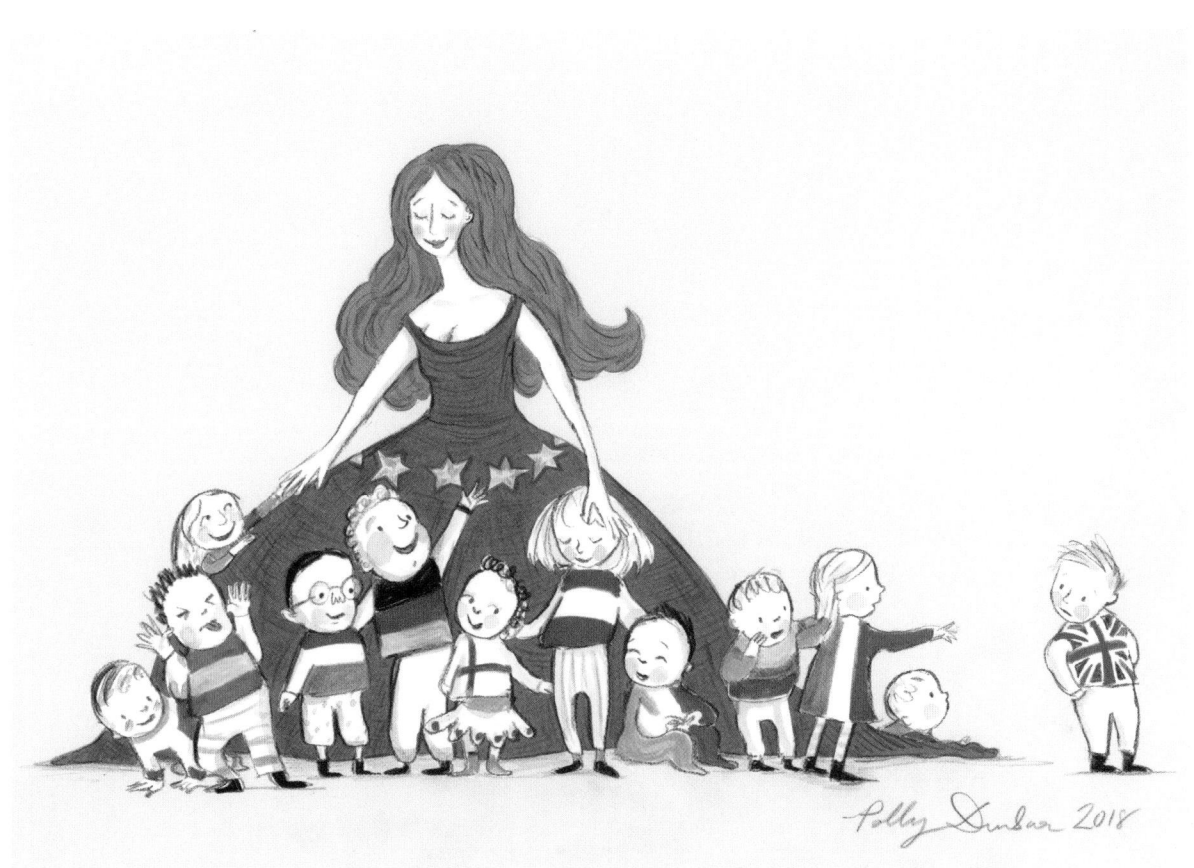

Lady Europa and Children

The children I drew are inspired by sketches of my son playing at home. I realize that he wouldn't be here were it not for the European Union. My husband and I met in London. We both came to study, work and live in the UK thanks to our Danish and French nationalities. London has become our home. I look at my baked-bean-loving son and I think of the different friendships, careers, adventures and families that have been made possible by the UK's membership of the European Union.

Emma Farrarons

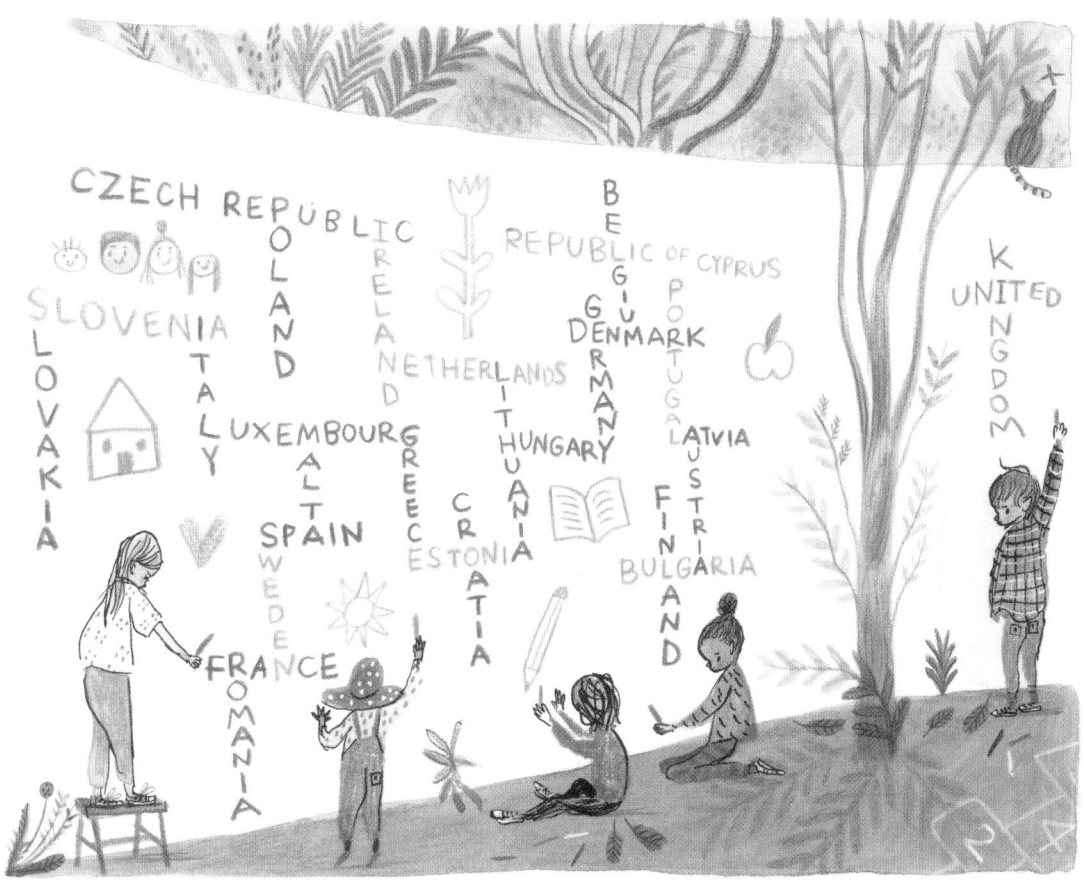

School Wall

I'm an English man who lives in France with my French wife and our young daughter. I moved to Paris three years ago following 'mon amour'. I was always proud of my country – Britain has long been seen as a creative, forward-thinking country – but the decision of Brexit is based on an ideology from the past.

'Hook a Duck' is a play on the EU flag as ducks. The British brolly hooking the duck is the old Britain destroying the unity of Europe. The calamitous Brexit seems to be people harking back to the old Britain; it's not forward thinking. It's destructive now, and for future generations.

I'm happy to be on this side of the Channel during this madness.

Jim Field

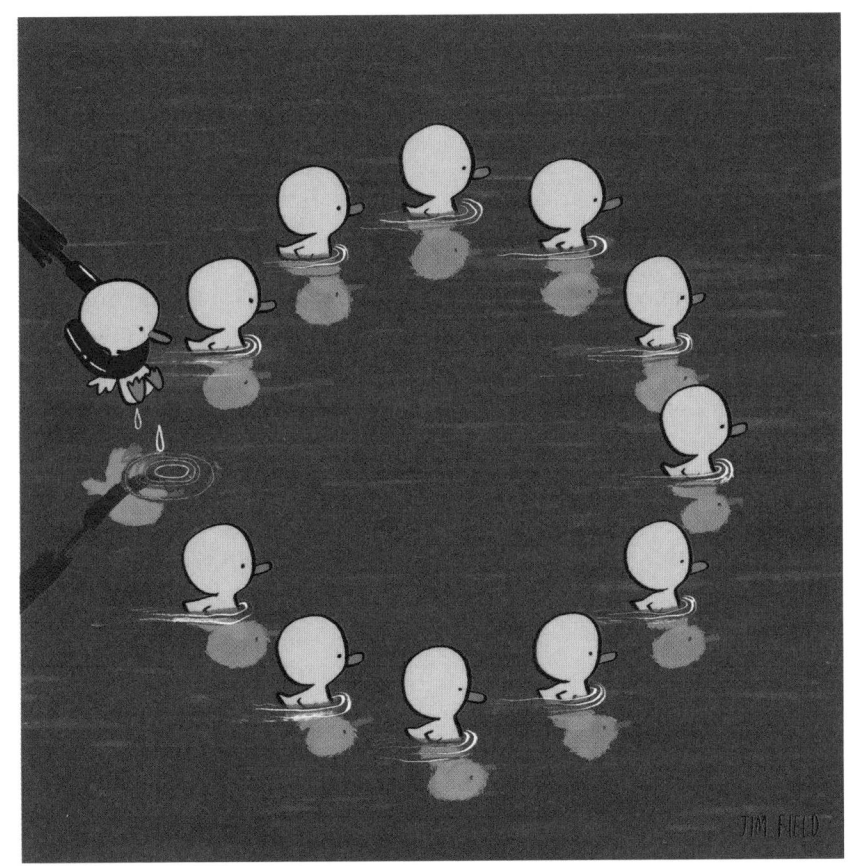

Hook a Duck

In my drawing I have imagined Victor Hugo in his writing room, composing the address he gave to the International Peace Conference held in Paris in 1849. I have used this quote to express my own hope for the future, and my hope that this dream will flourish again.

Tor Freeman

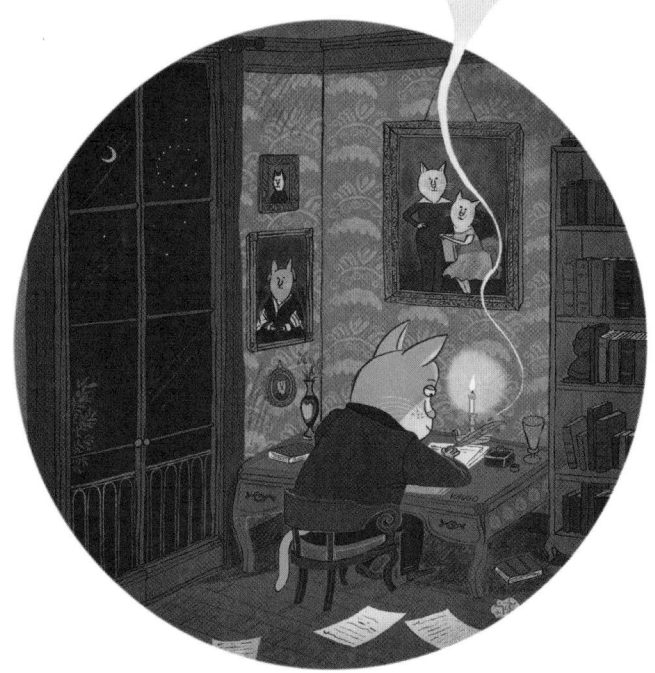

Stars

For me, the fact that so many different cultures live in such a small area in Europe and that we are now able to move and exchange so freely is a great enrichment: different landscapes, different foods, different ways of looking at things and different customs. This is fun and we can learn a lot from each other.

Katja Gehrmann

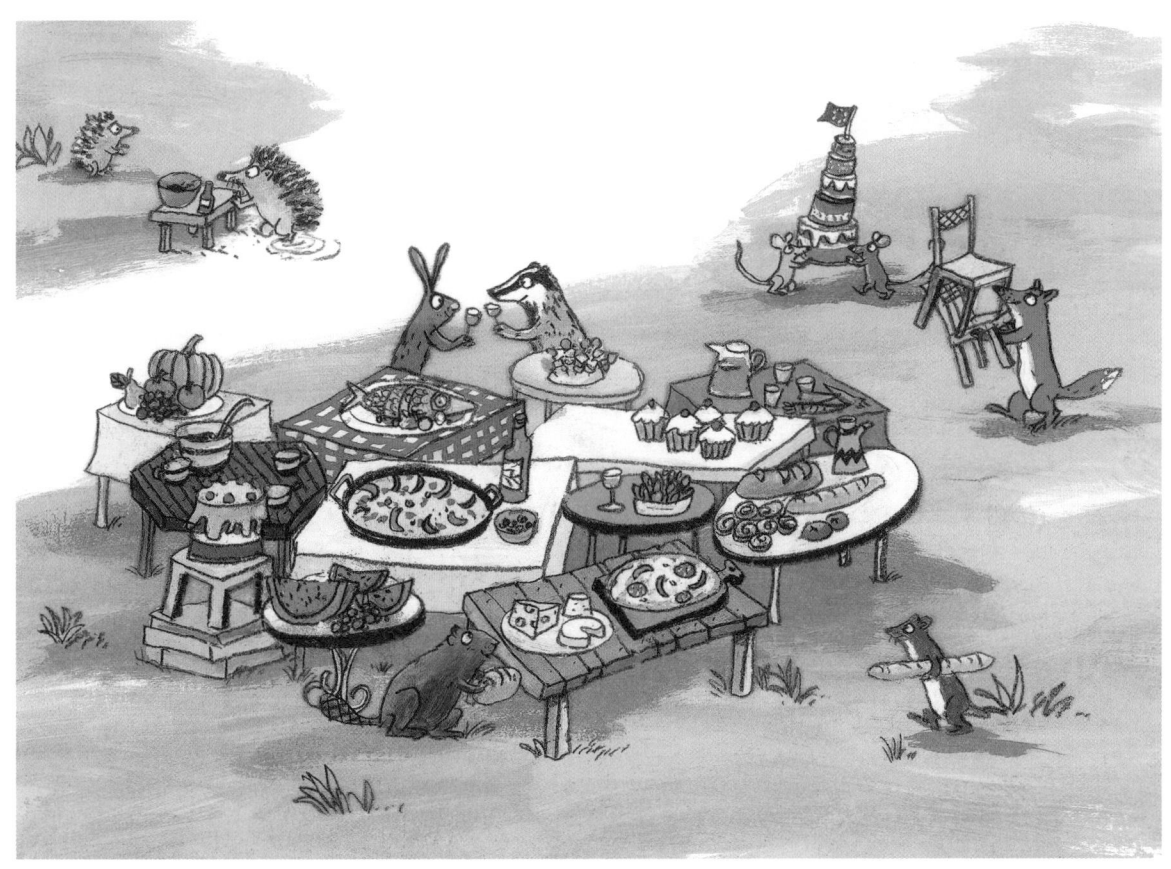

¡Viva Europa!

The balloon represents what we British have. No-one is allowed it except us. And now, after this ridiculous referendum, we're facing an uncertain future.

Patrick George

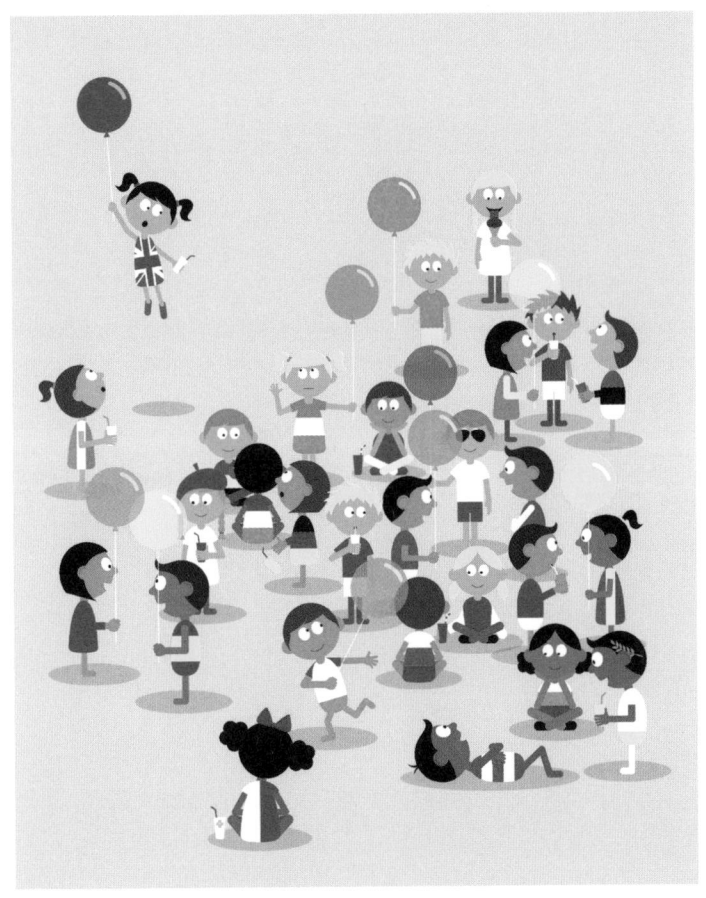

Let's Stick Together

I simply reversed the myth of Europa and the bull. For me, Europa is the one who leads the bull and shows it what it is all about. A little girl who is still naive and courageous.

Susanne Göhlich

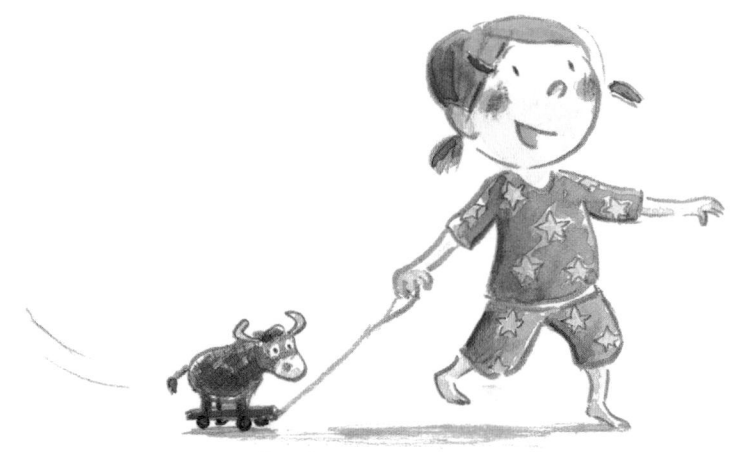

Lena als Europa mit dem Stier.
S.G. 2017

Lena as Europa with the Bull

No-one knows exactly what Brexit will mean for us all in the future. What saddens me is that it has already created division not just amongst nations, but neighbours and families too.

Emily Gravett

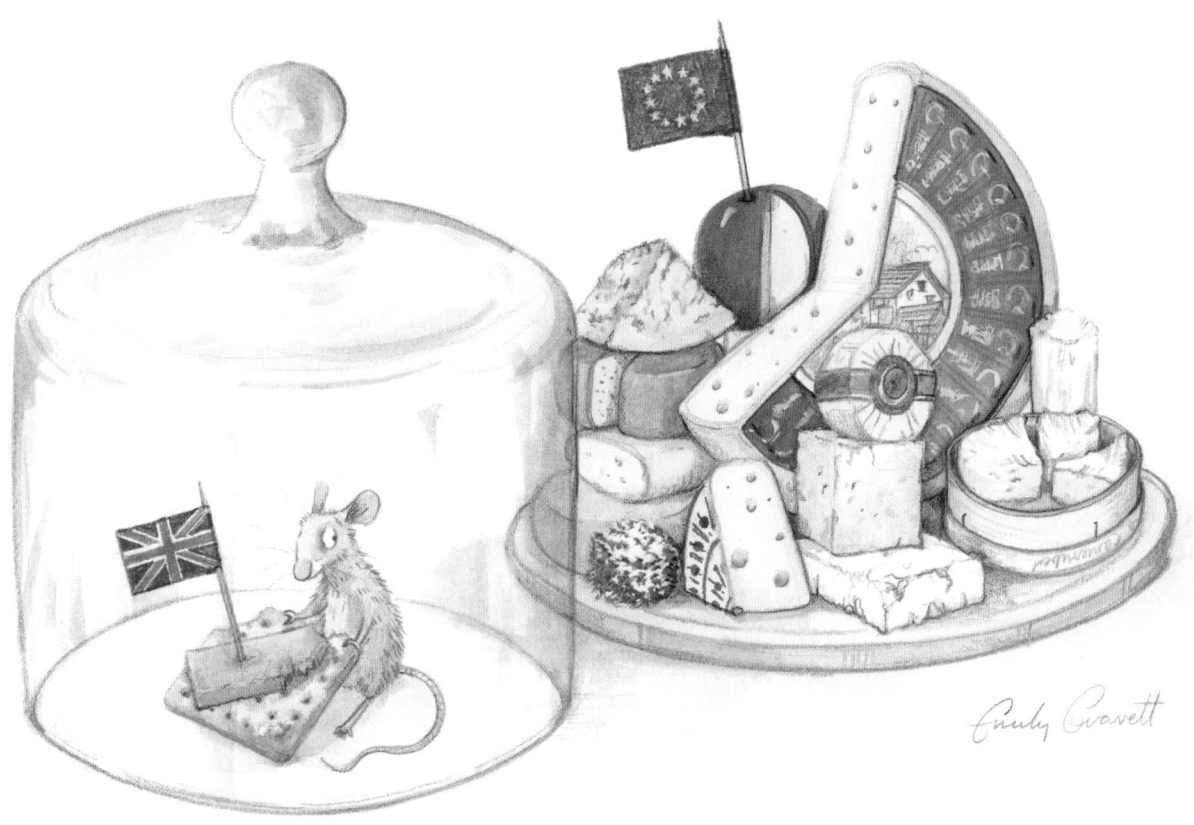

Britain Takes the Biscuit

There will always be a little corner of our umbrella to shelter a friend.

Aurélie Guillerey

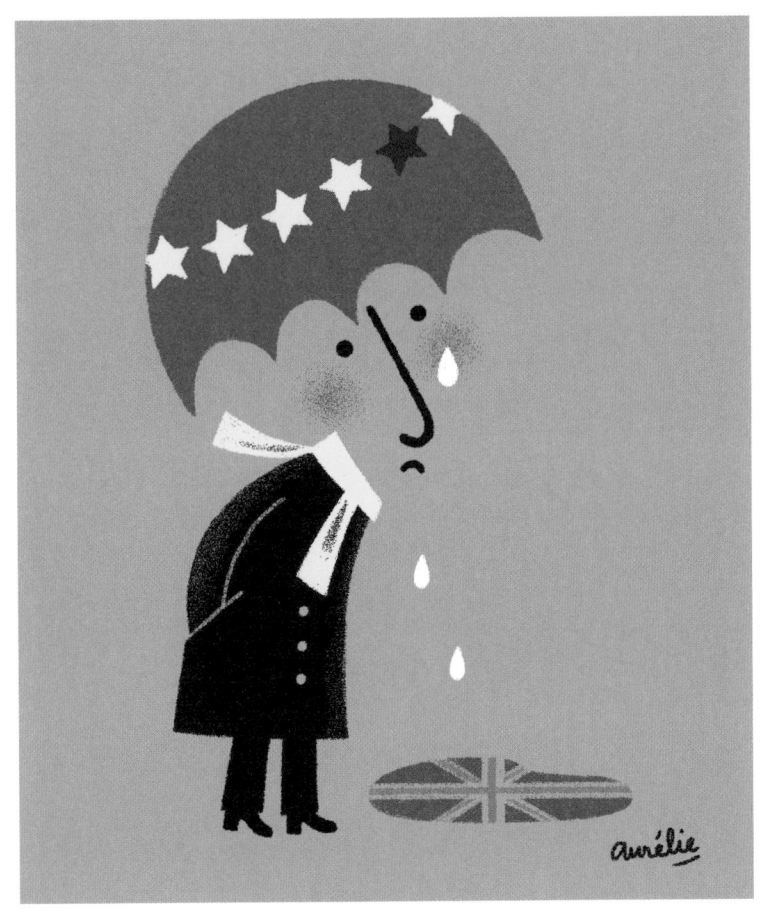

A Tear for Europe

I am Irish. I had lived and worked in many different countries before, but when I arrived in Hackney 15 years ago I found what I think is the best neighbourhood in the world. Some of the most talented people from across the world have all come to this one little place to work together. This area has more immigrants than almost any other borough in the UK and to me, that's what makes it magic. So I was saddened by the discussions around Brexit, and that others didn't feel the same way. When people with very different cultures and skills come together they create something unique. I emigrated to the UK because I wanted to contribute and do something with my work. I could never have made my books without moving to London first. We all came here because we want to contribute, to try to make something amazing together.

I created this image in the days before the Brexit vote to post on social media.

Chris Haughton

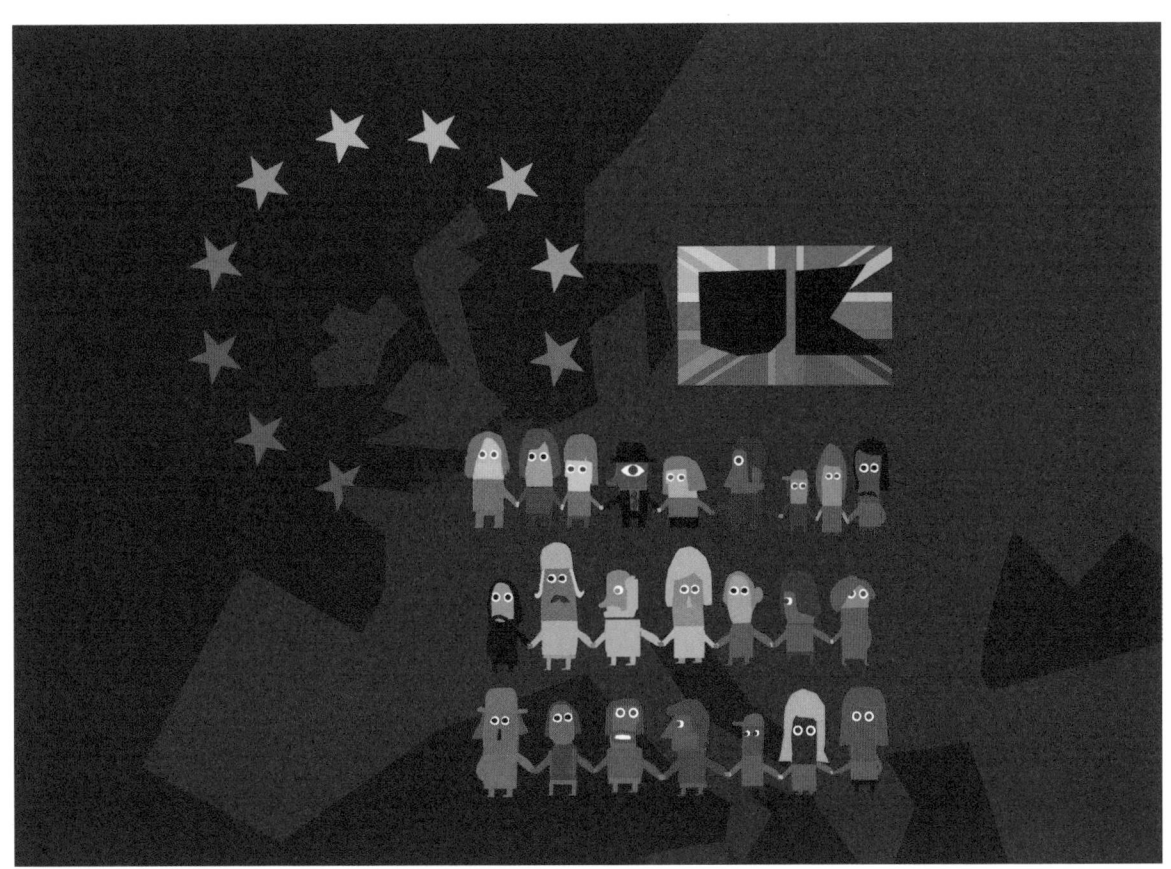

Vote Yes

Ours is much more than mine.

Morag Hood

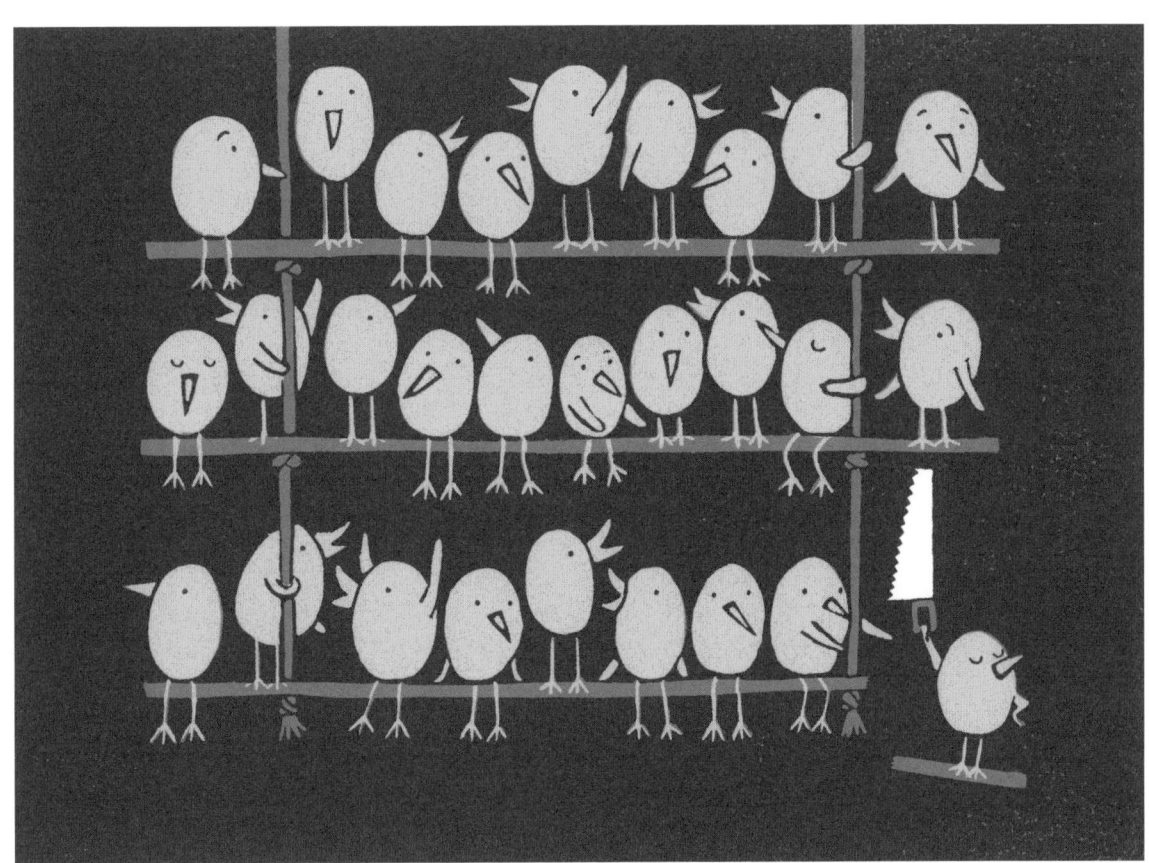

Divided

I really hope it is not too late and people come to their senses.
I love being a part of Europe and my children do too!

Bruce Ingman

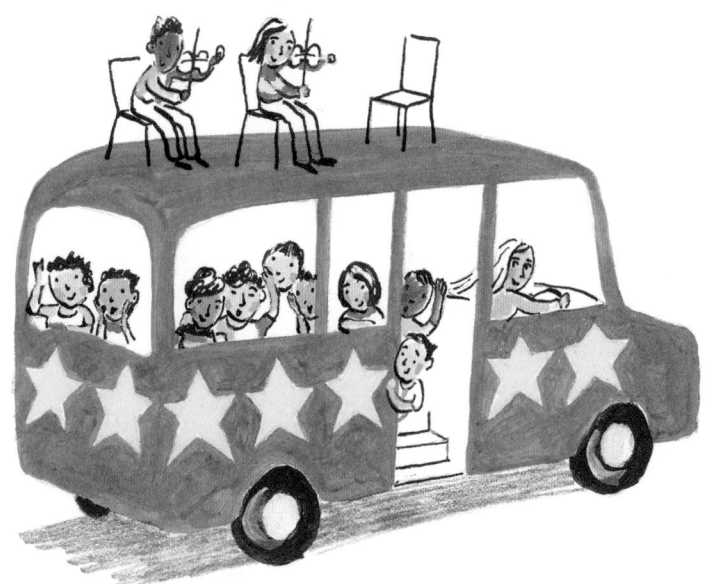

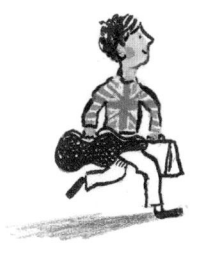

Hang On!

I love the UK. When I moved here from Ireland 15 years ago I felt thrilled to be part of such a progressive country.

Now a line has been drawn between 'us' and 'them'. And Brexit is a great big unknown. For the last two years, despite checking the news obsessively, I still have no idea what's going on. I am almost bored to tears with it.

However, there is always light. It's shining out of the faces of each person fighting for their friends, for togetherness; everyone who is invigorated by politics, and those learning how valuable our EU is. People are changing their hearts daily on Brexit. Whether you are 'Leave' or 'Remain', we need to understand each other. Don't let this divide us. Let's learn from this experience. Let's learn to love. It's not over yet.

Yasmeen Ismail

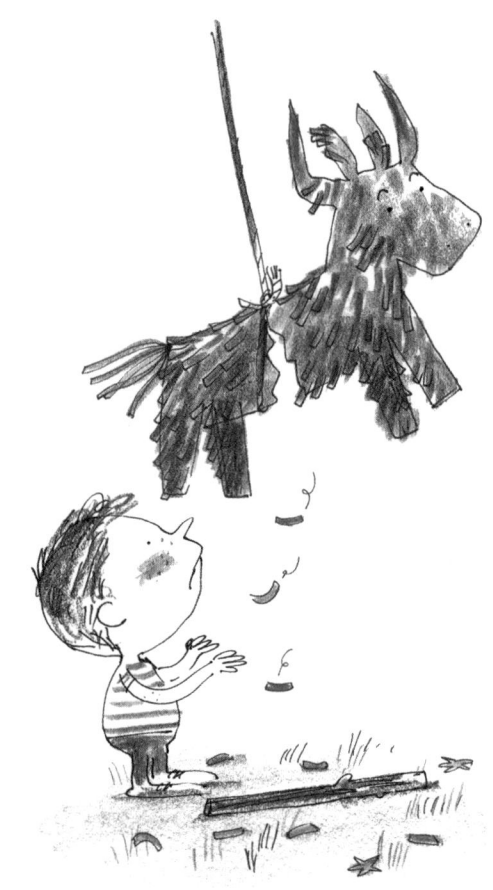

Brexit

The result of the Brexit vote throughout England and Wales was a sharp reminder to those of us living in Northern Ireland of how little we are thought of by those on the mainland. This work illustrates my current mindset of the soon-to-be British passport, and the uncertain consequences the vote may have on the already fragile peace upheld since the Good Friday agreement.

Oliver Jeffers

The STATELET OF THINGS

My Northern Irish Passport

Up Europe!

Judith Kerr

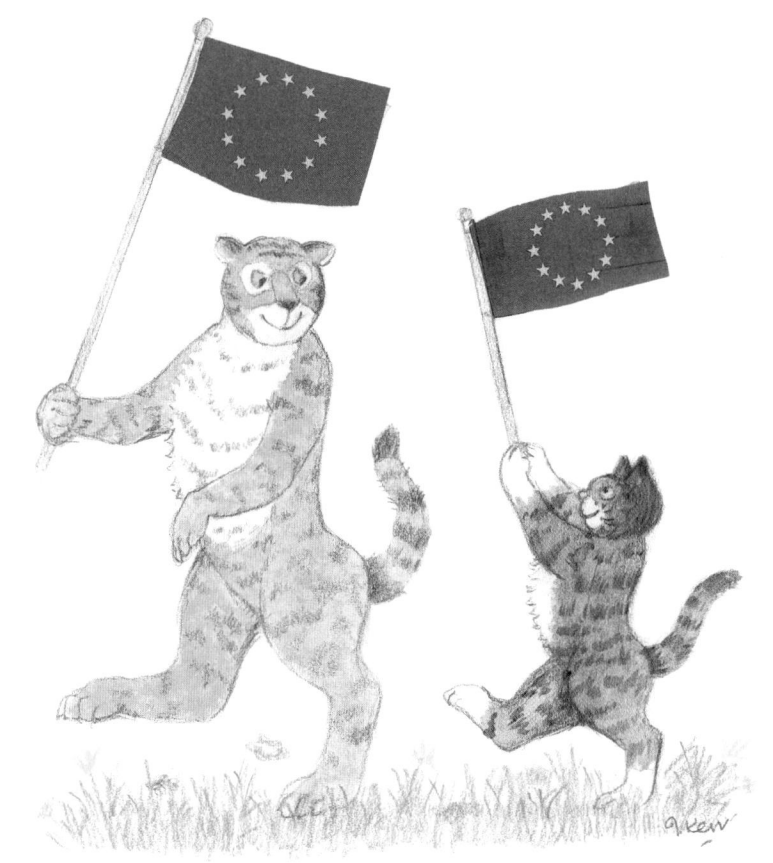

It was not easy to draw a positive propaganda piece on Europe. I only had bad ideas at first – and I thought I could not deliver a naked Europa. Then I found a bird's feather that I carved and drew her with. It made it somehow OK to draw a naked Europa. Think of what the bird has seen during its flight over the continent . . .

Ole Könnecke

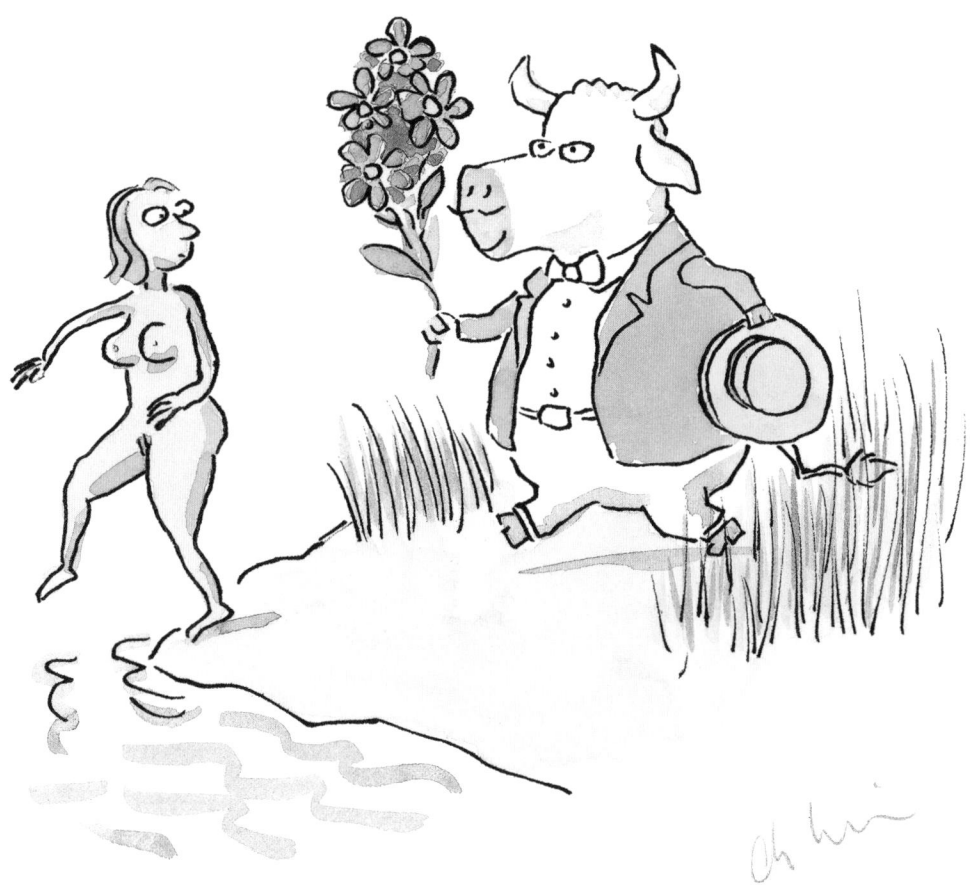

Europa is Bathing

I'm a British-born illustrator, and one of the 48% of Britons who didn't vote 'Leave'. In my illustration I wanted to show a void – a universe empty of stars. A 'U-turn' is the only option as I see it.

Neal Layton

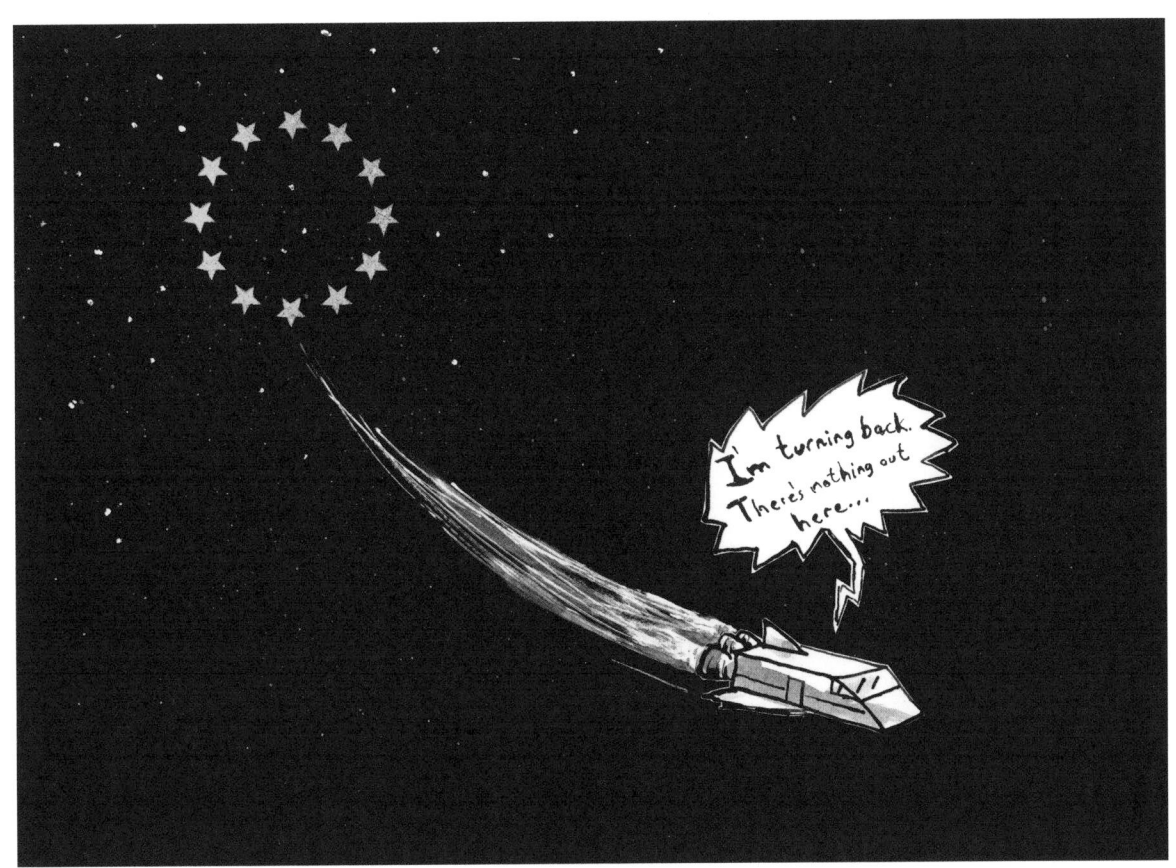

Mission Abort

Europe is beautiful and there are many sides to it. I've tried to get that across in these small pictures. I think that from a geographical point of view all countries are part of Europe – not just those that are part of the EU.

Sabine Lohf

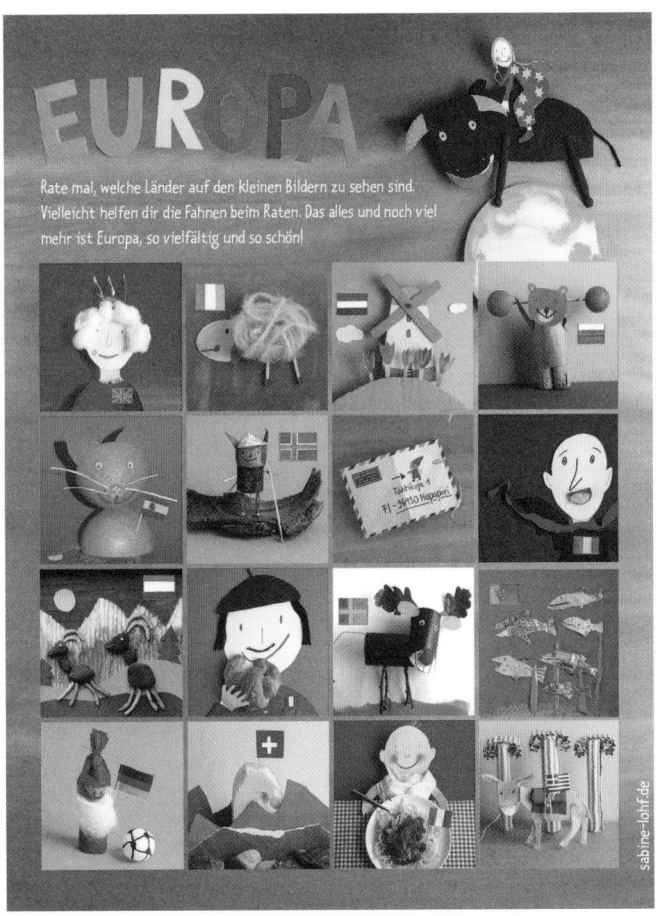

Europe – a Guessing Game

Children are Europe's future. As well as reading, writing and arithmetic, they should learn to play – just like I've played with the letters E, U, R, O, P and E here. It's an essential part of living together.

Édouard Manceau

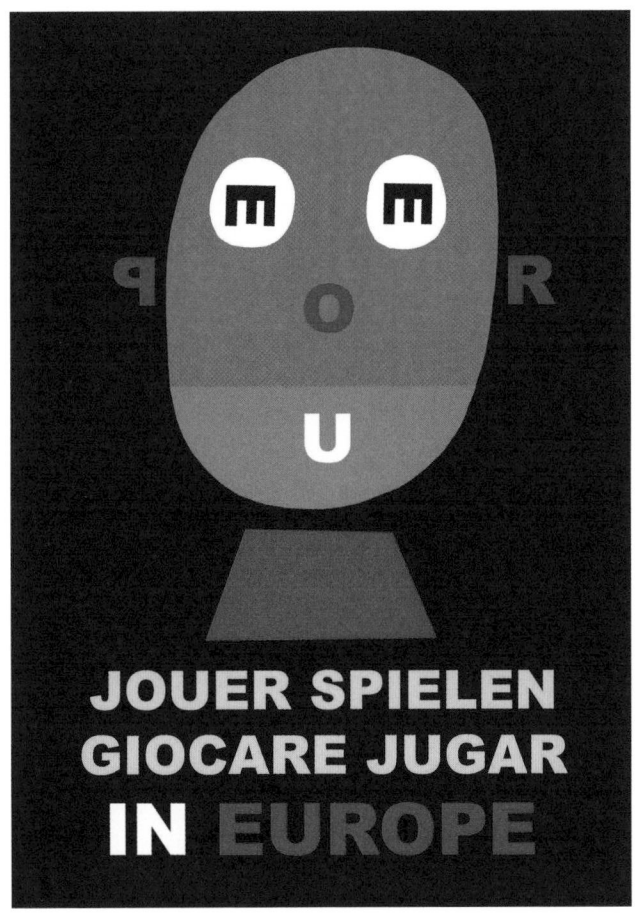

Playing en Europe

Twelve young 'stars' of Europe swing and climb around an autumnal tree. There's a solitary magpie in it too ('one for sorrow'). My young self looks on, unable to climb up. I feel as left out of the future of Europe as I felt as a child when I moved to a new school.

Bridget Marzo

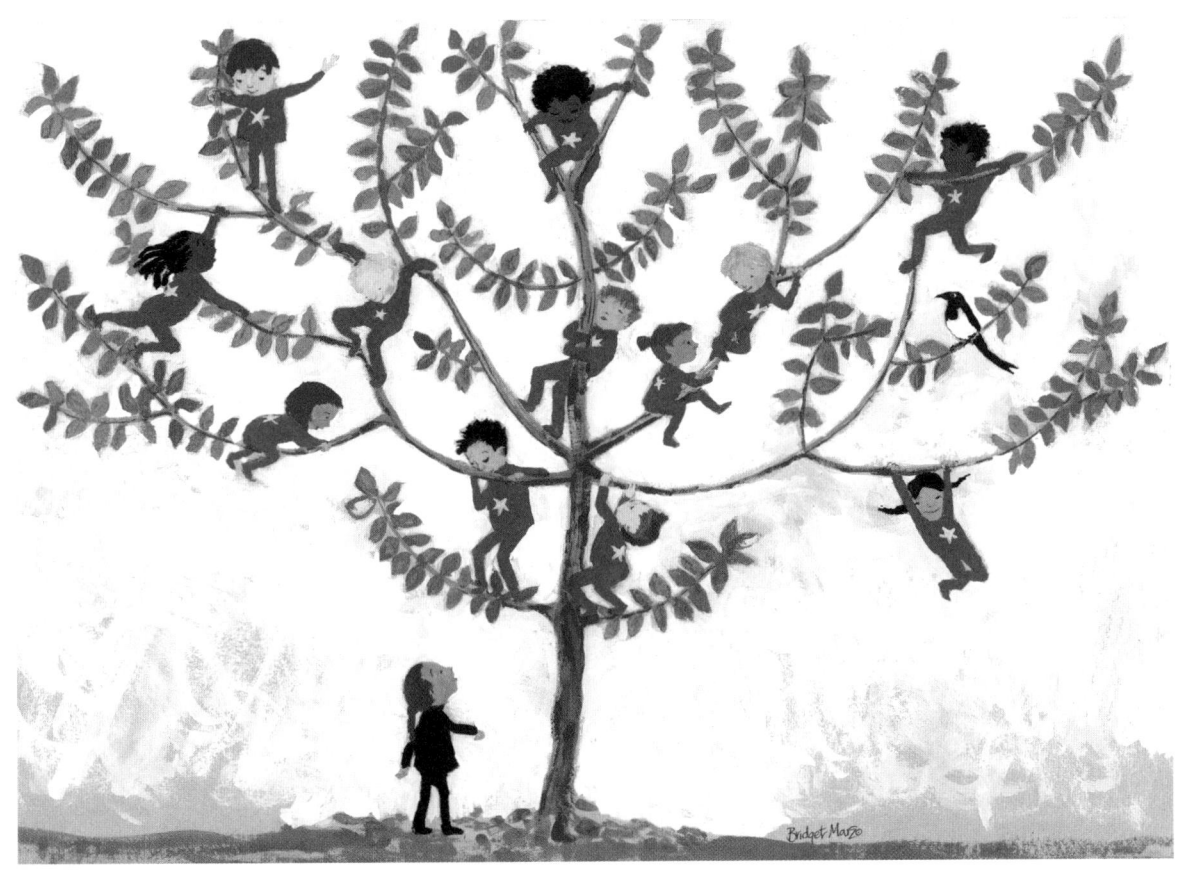

Europe in a Tree

My dad left Scotland as an economic migrant before I was born; I didn't realise I was an EU citizen until I was 18. When I found out, I was absolutely thrilled to get a passport that would let me live and work anywhere in Europe. Such freedom! It was like all my birthdays and Christmases rolled into one.

Sarah McIntyre

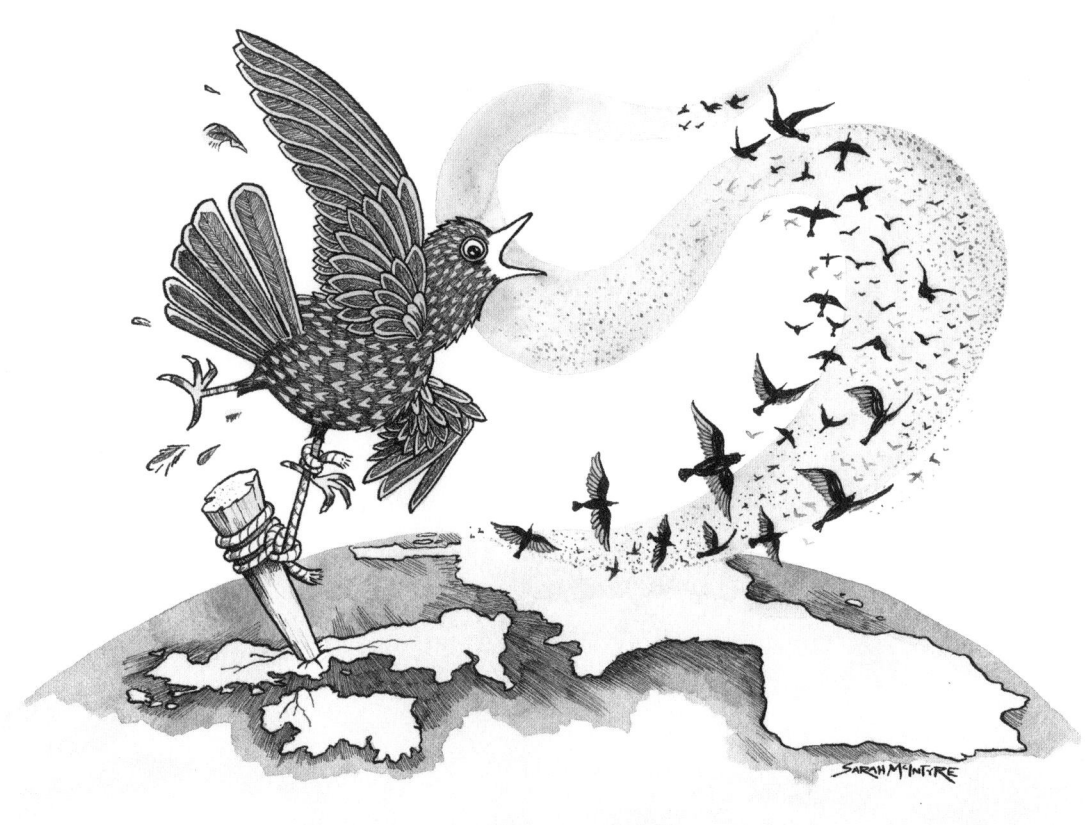

Murmuration of Starlings

Surely, it's always better to work in a team?

Lydia Monks

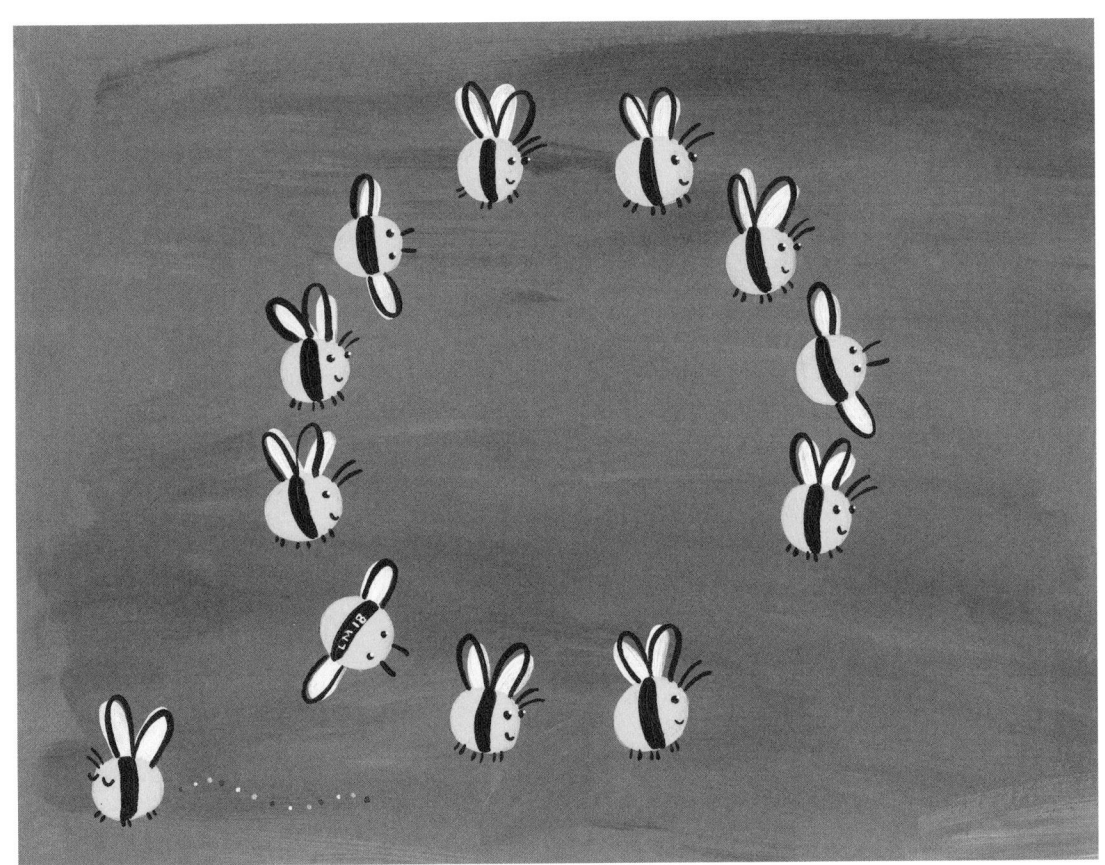

Bee Better Together

Unfortunately, for me it is much easier to make fun of something than praise it. So I had trouble finding my picture. Working in my own garden, I just thought of Europe as our little Garden of Paradise – a garden which must be looked after.

Jörg Mühle

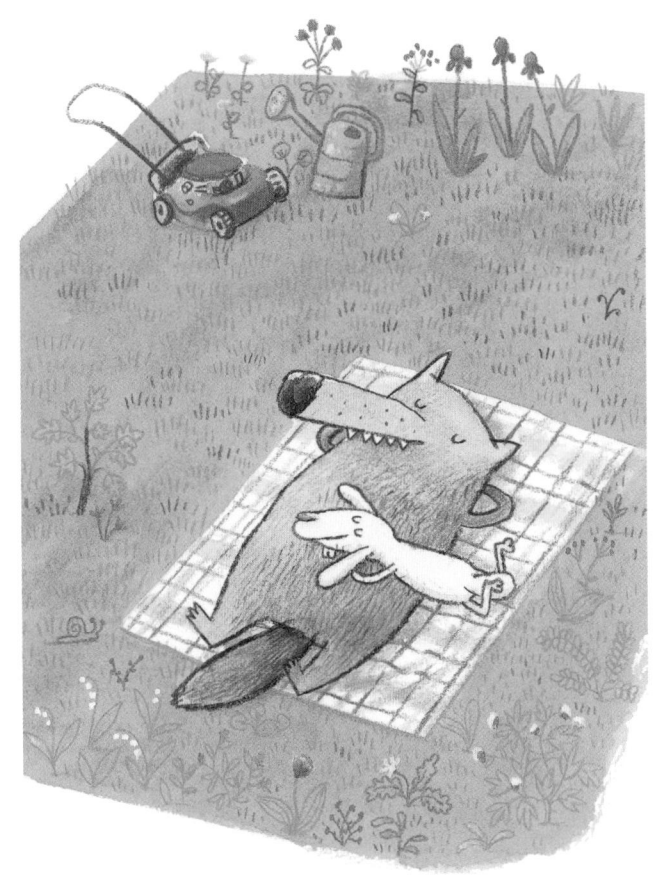

Europe – in the Garden of Paradise

The unification of Europe means overcoming division and separation. Walls, fences and barbed wire disappeared. Terrifying: now they are being rebuilt. A betrayal of Europe! Every effort and sacrifice will only be worthwhile if Europe remains a humane project.

Thomas Müller

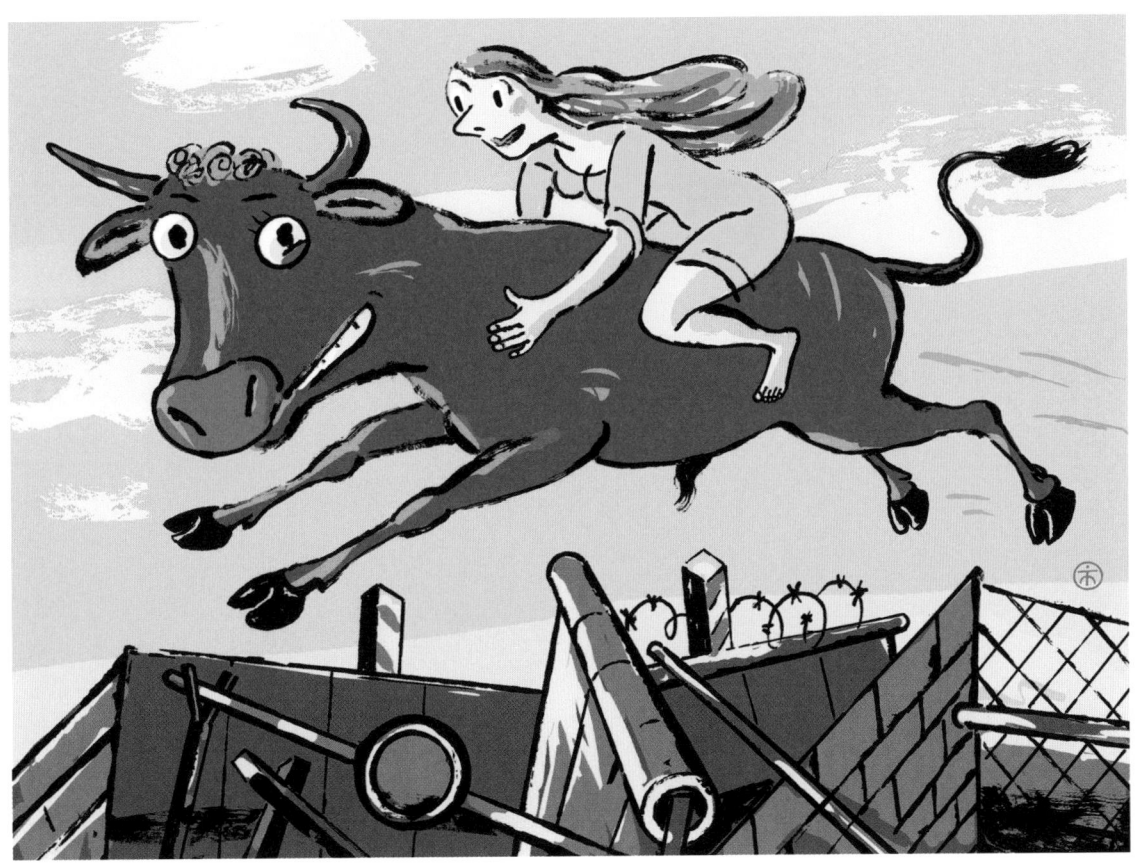

Europe Means Overcoming Division and Separation

Everyone can draw a personal diagram of any kind of connections (professional, family, love, sport, etc.) that one has to the countries and people of Europe. That would result in a different pattern for each of us. It is not the pattern that is important, but thinking about how you are personally connected with Europe in order to make such an identification conscious. 28 countries, connect yourself!

Andreas Német

28 Länder, bitte verbinden Sie selbst!

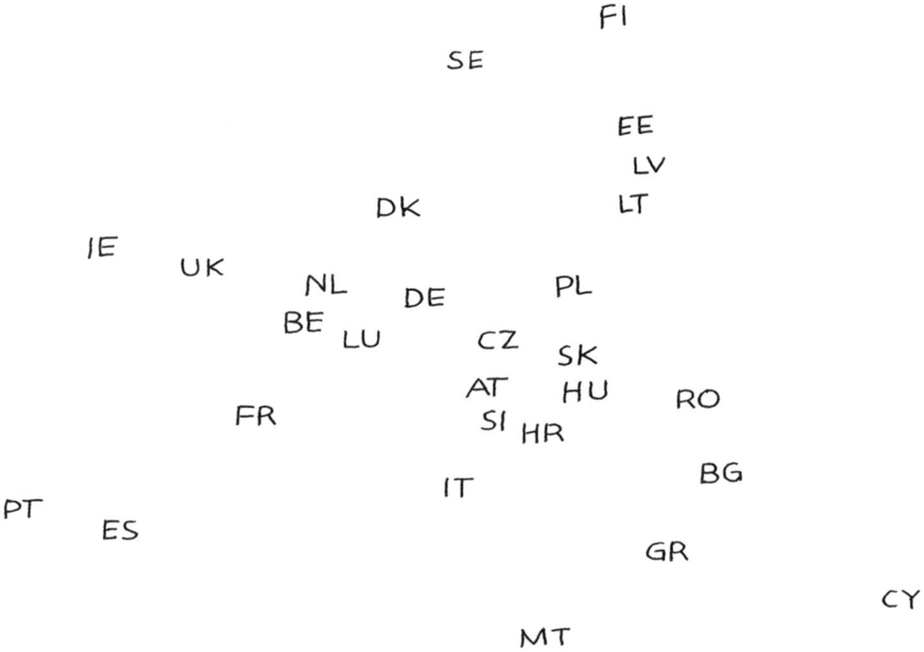

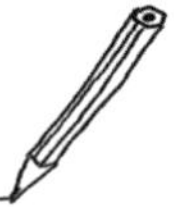

FI

SE

EE

LV

DK

LT

IE

UK

NL

DE

PL

BE

LU

CZ

SK

AT

HU

RO

FR

SI

HR

IT

BG

PT

ES

GR

CY

MT

And What Connections Do You Have to Europe?

As we move closer to EU departure, I'm increasingly concerned about what lies ahead. Brexit has turned lives upside down and caused divisions. I wanted to create an image that reflects Britain at this point in time – bobbing, disconnected, in a sea of uncertainty.

Sara Ogilvie

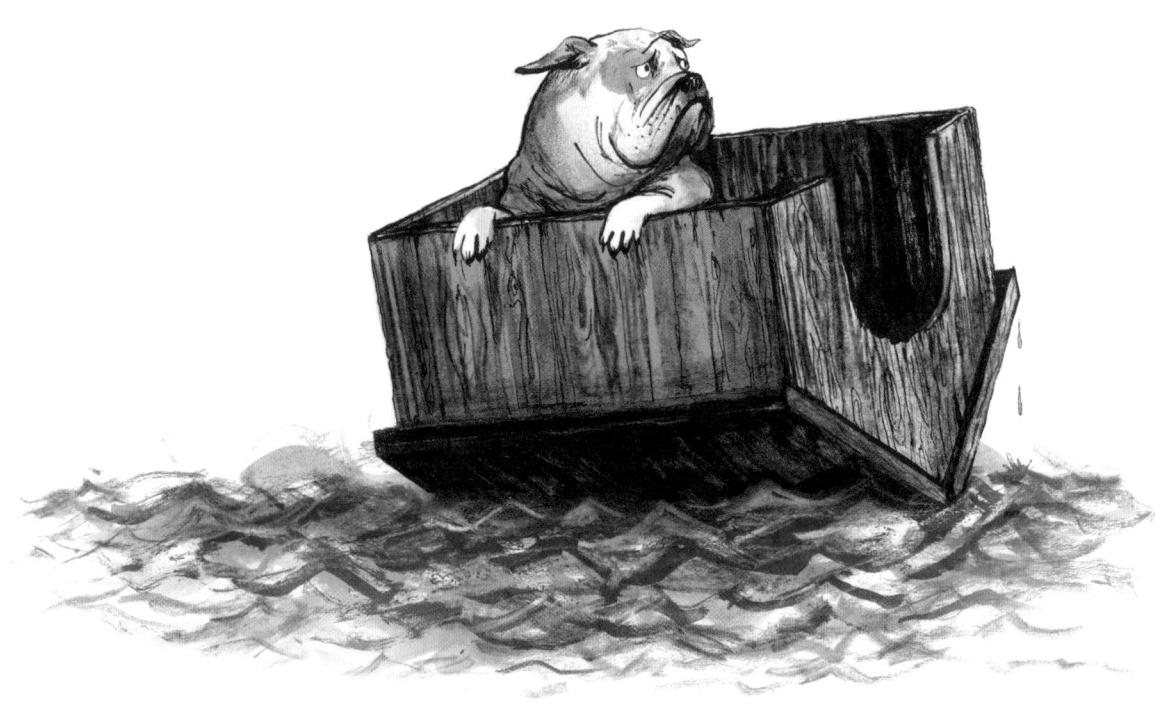

Adrift

Maeve could hardly believe her eyes. "Why on earth would you want to leave?" she squeaked.

But the butterfly carried on fluttering away, with its fragile and unstable wings.

It wasn't listening to a word that Maeve was saying.

Catherine Rayner

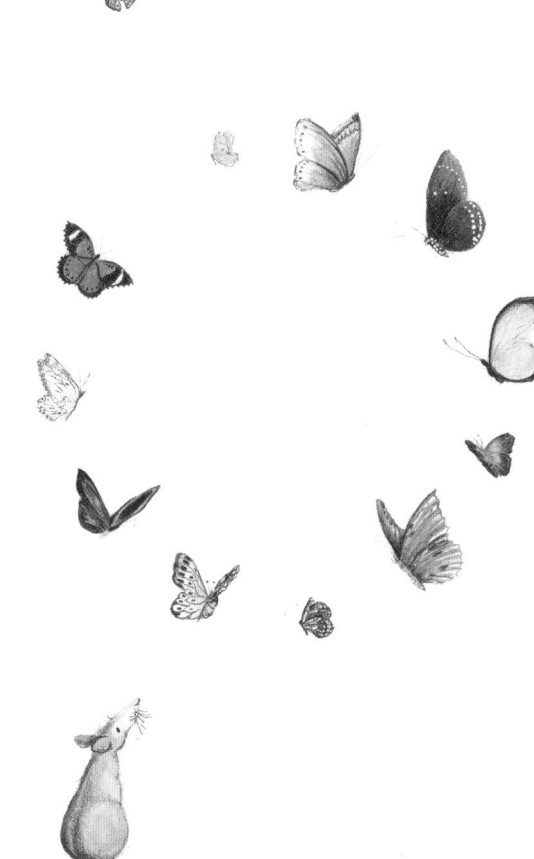

United in Diversity

The hard Brexit fantasists will be judged by future generations who will rightly ask why economic and cultural isolation was preferable to an ever-closer union. When we've had our fill of Turkish delight and permanent winter, there will be another referendum.

Chris Riddell

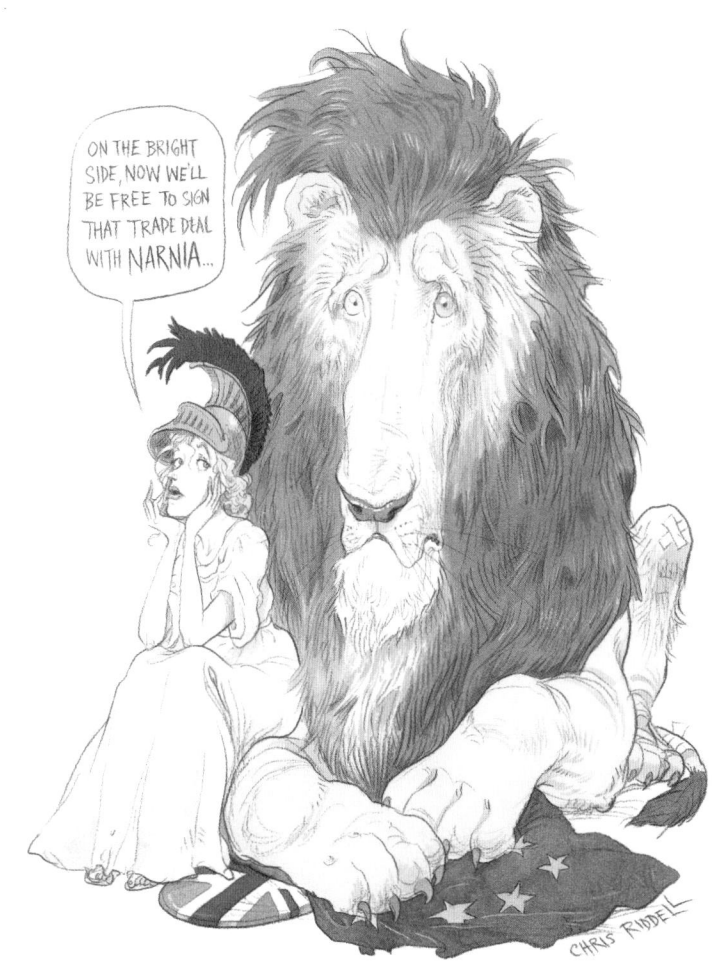

Narnia

It took me ages to think of what to draw! But I kept coming back to the image of the twelve gold stars on the European Union flag. They stand for unity, solidarity and harmony – the motto being 'united in diversity'. I likened it to a circle of friends enjoying a game. I thought about when one kid stops joining in with the game, how that affects the others in the group who are playing it: the game goes on but some kids might feel concerned, unsettled, sad, even annoyed that their friend has stopped playing.

David Roberts

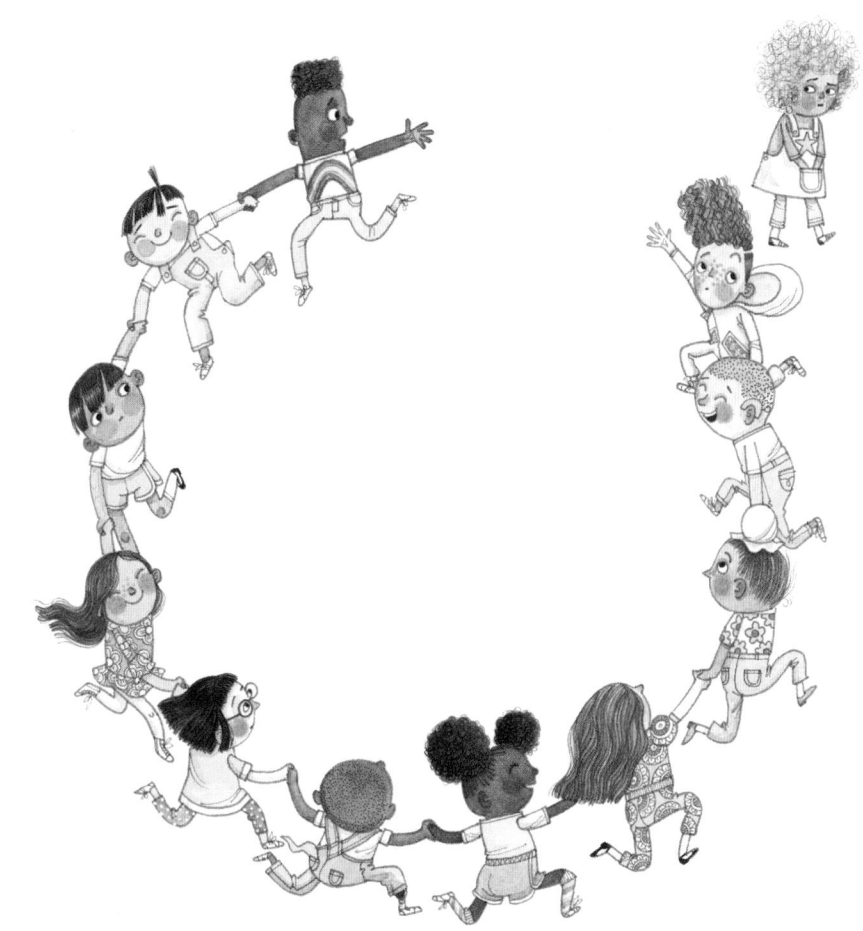

Not Playing

After an encounter with a British person who couldn't identify the European flag, I decided it was time for a child-friendly heraldic animal for the EU. I thought of an owl because it is a symbol of wisdom and of the Greek goddess Athena – and Greece was the cradle of Europe and of democracy. As I like owls very much anyway, I drew this one . . .

Axel Scheffler

*Eule (EU-le) is the German word for owl.

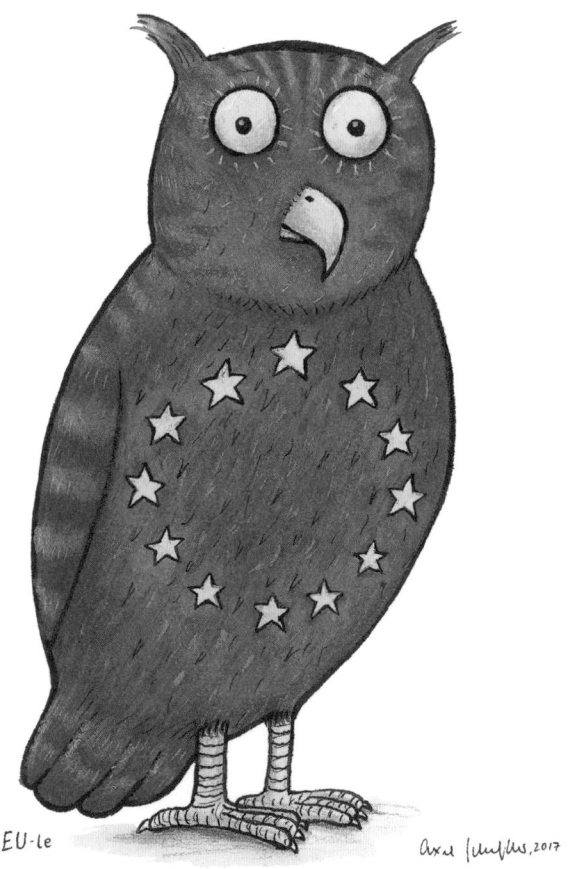

EU-le

Axel Scheffler, 2017

My Proposal for a European Heraldic Animal: the EU-le*

Many stars together in the night,
Help each other make the world bright.

Birgitta Sif

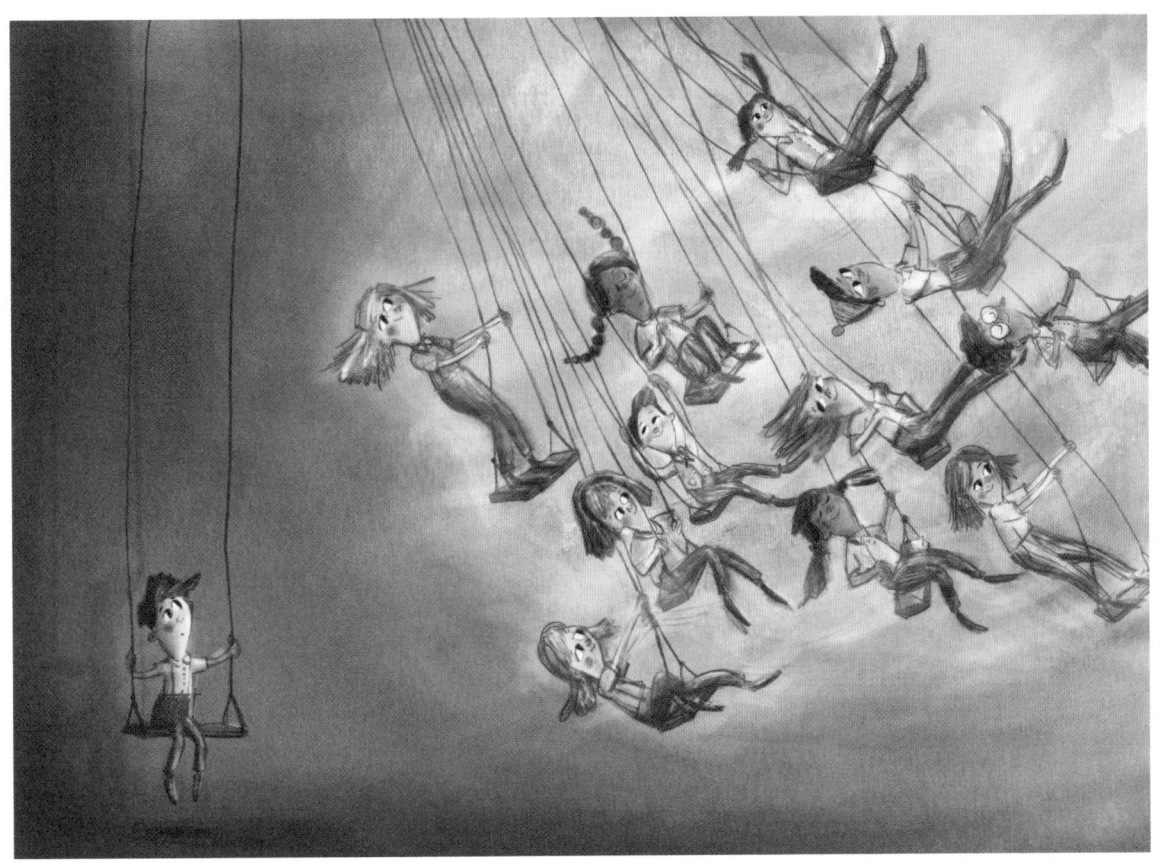

Stars

The European Union is a balancing act. My illustration is meant in a sarcastic way – everyone working together is just a dream. Making it actually happen is very difficult.

Thé Tjong-Khing

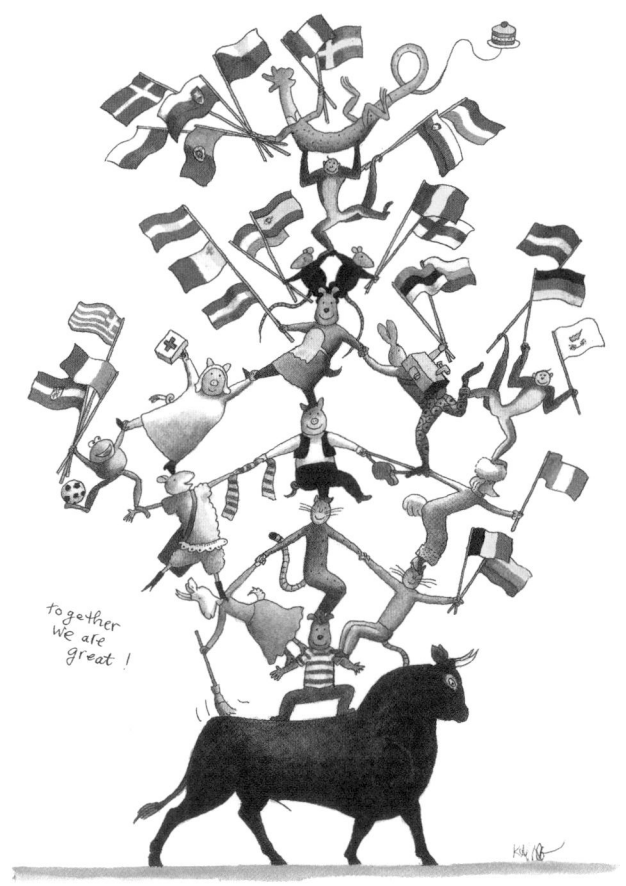

Together We Are Great!

Acknowledgments

The publishers would like to thank all forty-five illustrators for their contributions to this book.

Special thanks go to Liz Neville, Camille Ondet, Linda Owen-Lloyd, Axel Scheffler and Markus Weber.

The illustrations from the original 2017 exhibition have been auctioned to raise money for Pulse of Europe, an independent movement that aims to promote a new European awareness and consciousness that connects people and nations. www.pulseofeurope.eu